NEW DIRECTIONS FOR ADULT AND CONTINUING EDUCATION

Ralph G. Brockett, *University of Tennessee, Knoxville*
EDITOR-IN-CHIEF

Alan B. Knox, *University of Wisconsin, Madison*
CONSULTING EDITOR

Perspectives on Educational Certificate Programs

Margaret E. Holt
University of Georgia, Athens

George J. Lopos
University of Iowa, Iowa City

EDITORS

Number 52, Winter 1991

JOSSEY-BASS PUBLISHERS
San Francisco

PERSPECTIVES ON EDUCATIONAL CERTIFICATE PROGRAMS
Margaret E. Holt, George J. Lopos (eds.)
New Directions for Adult and Continuing Education, no. 52
Ralph G. Brockett, Editor-in-Chief
Alan B. Knox, Consulting Editor

Microfilm copies of issues and articles are available in 16mm and 35mm, as well as microfiche in 105mm, through University Microfilms Inc., 300 North Zeeb Road, Ann Arbor, Michigan 48106.

LC 85-644750   ISSN 0195-2242   ISBN 1-55542-766-9

NEW DIRECTIONS FOR ADULT AND CONTINUING EDUCATION is part of The Jossey-Bass Higher and Adult Education Series and is published quarterly by Jossey-Bass Publishers, 350 Sansome Street, San Francisco, California 94104-1310 (publication number USPS 493-930). Second-class postage paid at San Francisco, California, and at additional mailing offices. POSTMASTER: Send address changes to New Directions for Adult and Continuing Education, Jossey-Bass Publishers, 350 Sansome Street, San Francisco, California 94104-1310.

SUBSCRIPTIONS for 1991 cost $45.00 for individuals and $60.00 for institutions, agencies, and libraries.

EDITORIAL CORRESPONDENCE should be sent to the Editor-in-Chief, Ralph G. Brockett, Dept. of Technological and Adult Education, University of Tennessee, 402 Claxton Addition, Knoxville, Tennessee 37996-3400.

Cover photograph by Wernher Krutein/PHOTOVAULT © 1990.

Printed on acid-free paper in the United States of America.

CONTENTS

EDITORS' NOTES 1
Margaret E. Holt, George J. Lopos

1. A Rationale for Certificate Programs 3
Margaret E. Holt
A rationale for certificate programs is presented, supported by demographic data from the National Center for Education Statistics and from other studies and surveys. Certificate programs are defined and placed within the context of the larger arena of educational credentials.

2. Heuristics for Planning and Presenting Effective Certificate 11
Programs
Barry D. Bratton
Heuristics of certificate programs are discussed in terms of how they affect design, licensure, certification, and accreditation.

3. Evaluation and Quality Control in Certificate Programs 23
Mary Lindenstein Walshok
The issue of quality control in the development and delivery of certificate programs and the contribution of properly designed evaluations are addressed.

4. The Economics of Certificate Programs 33
Jane Hoopes Robinson
The costs involved in designing and providing certificate programs are examined in terms of direct expenses, staff, and institutional overhead. The discussion includes the income potential of this type of program, with full consideration of start-up and maintenance expenses.

5. Institutional Policies and Procedures: Bridges or Barriers? 43
John C. Snider, Francine Marasco, Donna Keene
Institutional policies and procedures that affect the development and implementation of certificate programs at traditional colleges and universities are examined. The aim is to help readers anticipate both potential institutional barriers to and sources of support for the development of certificate programs on their campuses.

6. Selected Interviews with Certificate Program Students 55
Thomas M. Rutkowski, Margaret E. Holt, George J. Lopos
The motivations and experiences of participants in career and personal development certificate programs are described. Consumers' reactions to many of the issues addressed in the previous chapters are presented, based on interviews with selected individuals who have completed certificate programs.

7. An Institutional History of Certificate Programs at George   63
Washington University
Abbie O. Smith

The history of certificate programs at George Washington University is examined and the characteristics and motivations of program participants are described.

8. Certification Programs for Business and Industry   77
Theodore J. Settle

Certification programs developed for business and industry and reasons for providing in-house certification programs are described.

9. Certificate Programs: Alternative Ways to Career Advancement   87
and Social Mobility?
George J. Lopos

The issues presented in the previous chapters are reviewed and synthesized. The author also describes additional resources for information about certificate programs and considers the societal implications of certificate programs.

INDEX   99

EDITORS' NOTES

The system of degrees and academic credentials found in American colleges and universities traces its lineage back to the guilds of Bologna, Italy, the medieval German universities, and the great English universities of Oxford and Cambridge. With some adaptations, this system of bachelor's, master's, and doctoral degrees defines the way that American colleges and universities differentiate among levels of academic preparation. By contrast, nondegree education in the United States traces its lineage to a more indigenous educational landscape: professional school education, egalitarian notions in formal education, the bureaucracy of American education, and even consumer protection.

This volume, *Perspectives on Educational Certificate Programs,* presents a variety of topics central to the understanding and implementation of certificate programs. The first chapter (Holt) describes the purpose of certificate programs in the current educational scene. The next four chapters address the formal qualities of certificate programs and practical questions involved in creating successful programs. Issues of formal instructional design (Bratton), evaluation and quality control (Walshok), economics (Robinson), and institutional environment (Snider, Marasco, and Keene) guide the reader through a brief tutorial on the development of certificate programs.

The next section of the volume broadens the perspective beyond formal considerations by providing illustrations of certificate programs and their outcomes. Two chapters provide a consumer's perspective on certificate programs, one from the perspective of program graduates (Rutkowski, Holt, and Lopos) and one from the perspective of business and industry (Settle), and one chapter (Smith) provides an institutional history. The final chapter (Lopos) summarizes the volume, cites several additional resources for information about certificate programs, and considers the role of certificate programs as part of a new paradigm for colleges and universities and as a mechanism for social mobility.

Margaret E. Holt
George J. Lopos
Editors

Margaret E. Holt is associate professor of adult education at the University of Georgia, Athens, and she is an associate with the Charles F. Kettering Foundation in Dayton, Ohio.

George J. Lopos is associate dean of continuing education at the University of Iowa, Iowa City. He has served on the National University Continuing Education Association Board of Directors and as chair of its Division of Special Certificates and Degree Programs. He co-edited Peterson's Guide to Certificate Programs in American Colleges and Universities *(Princeton, N.J.: Peterson's Guides, 1988).*

Certificate programs began to flourish in the 1970s as a response to specific technological and professional demands for concise and concentrated studies.

A Rationale for Certificate Programs

Margaret E. Holt

Studies describing certificate programs in the United States present limited information about their historical development. Smith (1987) observed that credit and noncredit work-related programs were first offered in the late 1940s by American colleges and universities. College and university brochures and other program promotional materials from the early 1970s define this period as one in which an increasing number of career-related programs of study officially called certificate programs were established in academic institutions.

The relationship of the majority of these programs to the demands of a more technical and specialized work force is readily documented. In a 1987 speech to the South Regional Conference of the American Association of University Students, Joseph Hankin, president of Westchester Community College in Valhalla, New York, talked about the future of higher education and, in part, explained the growth in certificate programs in some colleges and universities. He observed that the trend is for education to become more practical and more relevant: "Education cannot be isolated from the subject matter of life. . . . We cannot overlook the necessity of providing upgrading and retraining to the dislocated workers whose jobs have changed and who need additional education just to keep abreast, or to change fields" (Hankin, 1988, p. 303). He predicted that educational institutions will not be sites from which individuals "graduate" but instead places to which individuals repeatedly return to retool, advance, divert into other areas, or pursue leisure studies.

One measure of the accuracy of Hankin's remarks is the range of professional needs that has motivated the development of certificate programs. It is not uncommon for certificate programs to be requested by employers, professional associations, and accrediting, certifying, and licensing agencies, who then collaborate in their design and development. Occasionally, certificate programs are prerequisites for individuals who wish to take professional examinations for licensure in their respective fields. The certified financial planner program described by Settle (this volume) is an example of a certificate program that relates to licensure in a profession. In fact, some professional associations recognize all or part of certificate program courses in granting continuing education units.

Although diverse in content areas, certificate programs have certain features in common. The programs focus on areas of specialized knowledge or information and contain a number of courses and hours to meet the occupational, professional, or personal improvement needs of well-defined audiences. If a program is noncredit, its length is not determined by the traditional formula of contact hours per credit hour, and therefore it does not use the designations of credit hour courses. The program may not even use continuing education units but instead maintain its own integrity as defined by a program of study and evaluation. As with traditional degree and specialty programs, institutions have sole responsibility for determining the academic level at which the programs are offered. This means that some certificate programs are baccalaureate level, others are postbaccalaureate, and still others are graduate level. My intention here is to more clearly define and describe certificate programs as they are evolving and expanding in the United States by considering both their development and use. The common as well as unique characteristics of the programs, especially as they relate to other programs in higher education contexts, are identified. Finally, issues of quality and credibility are discussed.

Defining Certificate Programs

As they have grown in popularity, certificate programs understandably have been scrutinized by a skeptical academic establishment in its effort to find a niche for this mode of learning within the traditional structures of higher education. The definition of certificate programs continues to evolve, as do the institutional practices and academic policies related to them. Generally, this evolution has been guided by the academic standards and administrative procedures that define traditional degrees. In certain colleges and universities, the numbers of certificate programs have expanded rapidly, while other institutions have reluctantly added "nontraditional" and "nondegree" certificate offerings. Both the credit and the noncredit programs have their adherents. Undoubtedly, there are places that advocate certificate programs as a way to challenge certain principles and practices of traditional degree programs, such as graduate and undergraduate program approval and implementation policies and procedures. For purposes of discussion here, certificate programs are defined as programs at accredited colleges or universities that constitute a sequence, pattern, or group of courses developed, administered, and evaluated by faculty or faculty-approved professionals. Further, such programs, regardless of whether they are credit or noncredit, are officially approved by academic officers.

As noted earlier, information about the development of certificate programs in American colleges and universities is sparse. Smith (1987) conducted a computerized search of the literature and found only two studies of certificate programs. A computer search that I made of *Dissertation Abstracts International* for the period January 1987 through December 1989 found only twelve dissertations with the words "certificate programs" in the abstracts. None contained these words in the titles. In two of the studies, certificate programs were only mentioned in the findings sections, where they were identified as recommendations to educational institutions (for example, community colleges) for expanding programs and contributing to the economic viability of organizations. A related search of education abstracts over a seven-year period (1983–1990) likewise was not productive in terms of information on the general status of certificate programs. However, the number of citations related to community and junior colleges suggests that investigations of certificate programs in these institutional settings might uncover rich sources of details on program characteristics.

The 1987 survey used to prepare *Peterson's Guide to Certificate Programs at American Colleges and Universities* (Lopos, Holt, Bohlander, and Wells, 1988) revealed that there are two major objectives of certificate programs at accredited colleges and universities: self-enrichment and, accounting for the greatest number of existing programs in recent years, career enhancement. Law, business, and accounting programs, in particular, were the top three curricular areas for these programs. Other popular career programs identified by this survey were paralegal training, human resources development, health and health-related fields, personnel administration, computer programming, and business management. Similarly, the National Center for Education Statistics (Carpenter, 1989) ranked college and university certificate enrollments for 1986–87 as follows: (1) business and management, (2) education, (3) theology, (4) health sciences, (5) liberal/general studies, (6) social sciences, (7) multi- and interdisciplinary studies, tied with psychology, (8) computer/information sciences, (9) law, and (10) allied health.

The paralegal and legal assistant programs illustrate academic institutions' response to a rapidly growing employment field. National news media, for example, identified this area as the fastest growing employment field of the 1980s. The types of certificate programs available reflect the increasing specialization of career areas in society: filmmaking, alcohol and drug counseling, foreign language translation, book publishing, fundraising management, travel and tourism, international banking, software engineering, and light systems design. These courses represent only a small segment of programs offered around the country.

Academic, Governmental, and Business Responses to Certificate Programs

Expansion in areas of employment has promoted the development of certificate programs. At George Washington University, for example, a pioneer institution in the development of certificate programs (see Smith, this volume), most of the programs resulted from an increasing need for employees in emerging careers such as paralegal assistance. Generally, traditional degree programs either were not available to satisfy employers' needs for particular types of skills and expertise or were not offered at times convenient to employers and students. Columbia University has recognized that persons prepared in certain fields with currently limited employment opportunities may be able to add completion of a certificate program to their resumés and become more marketable candidates for positions (Gordon, 1987). The university's "Elements of Digital Computer Technology" is a course requirement in a three-semester certificate program developed specifically to ready students in other fields for new careers in business data processing.

As college and university administrators, faculty, students, and potential employers have become aware of jobs that demand concentrated study, they have tailored old and designed new programs to mutually serve their institutions, communities, and businesses. Almost all of the programs identified by Smith (this volume) and Settle (this volume) can be linked to technological, economic, or legal demands in emerging career areas.

States continue to legislate the upgrading of professional credentials, while competition and economic pressures cause employers to seek employees with specializations. In some instances, individuals are not eligible to take an examination for a professional license until they have successfully completed a certificate program. Real estate and insurance brokerage are good examples of careers where certificate programs are prerequisites for taking the licensing examinations. These kinds of professional eligibility requirements in part explain why certain academic institutions have developed the certificate as an alternative credential to traditional degrees.

The term *certificate program* is not synonymous with accreditation, certification, or licensure, which denote legal or professional rights to practice. Accreditation is a voluntary process by which an independent agency grants recognition to an education program or institution. Certification is a voluntary process by which an independent agency recognizes the competence of an individual. Licensure, however, is a mandatory process by which the government permits individuals to practice in designated professions. Its primary purpose is to protect the public from incompetent practitioners (Gilley and Gailbraith, 1987).

At best, completion of certificate programs means that individuals have acquired certain proficiencies in concentrated areas of study. The term *proficiencies* is used here with the same meaning as articulated in Gonnella and Zeleznik (1983, p. 61): "The goal of continuing professional education is to ensure the development of proficiencies that can be translated into professional performance. Properly speaking, then, education is connected not to performance but to proficiency." Phillips (1987, p. 5) further clarifies this distinction between proficiency and performance by noting, "Proficiencies are viewed as skills, knowledge, and experiences possessed by individuals. Performance is the outcome of how those proficiencies are used. Proficiencies are a means to an end, the end being performance." The content of most certificate programs is practical rather than theoretical, since the rationale for the study is most frequently immediate application of such skills, knowledge, and experiences in a work setting. Independent agencies and governmental bodies may determine that certificate programs are required for certification, accreditation, or licensure, but this is not the case for many programs that have been developed to address specific technological and professional demands.

A promotional piece from the University of California-Berkeley Extension/Business and Management responds succinctly to the question "Why do people want to earn certificates?": (1) to acquire additional job skills, (2) to justify promotion, (3) to prepare for a new career, (4) as proof of concentrated study, (5) for professional updating, (6) for second-income potential, (7) not interested in pursuing a formal degree, (8) to examine a new field, (9) to expand opportunities in the business world, and (10) to meet others with the same professional interests. Although some people may not be interested in pursuing a formal degree, certain certificate programs are designed to provide opportunities for individuals to "experiment" with a new field before deciding whether or not they want a formal degree program. When familiarization in a field is one of the purposes of a certificate program, providers often arrange for credits to be transferred later into the degree program. In describing guidelines for the development of certificate programs, one academic manager noted that "another criteria [sic] we have attempted to keep in mind in credit certificate programs has been the concept that they should provide a 'step up to commitment' to a degree program" (Shirley Smith Hendrick, letter to the author, May 5, 1986).

Data describing participants enrolled in certificate programs most frequently show that these individuals have already completed college degrees or have some college experience (Smith, 1987). Personnel already engaged in careers who need additional instruction in their fields or in new fields report a variety of advantages of certificate programs. Examples of such benefits are concentration on specialized knowledge or information in a condensed time period, flexible scheduling, low tuition costs, greater identification with fellow students, and valuable networking opportunities (Smith, 1987).

Institutions with substantial experience in managing certificate programs have gone through developmental processes in their course offerings. That is, after completing basic certificate programs, professionals have encouraged institutions to create more advanced programs. While some programs are suitable for both novices and established professionals, others define levels according to prior education and work experiences. Again, the experiences in developing a large number of certificate programs at George Washington University, beginning with the first in 1972, evidence the evolving nature of such programs.

Occasionally, academic institutions have determined that employment sites are preferable settings for these programs or in other ways have collaborated with corporations and other providers to offer these programs. A number of certificate programs are offered through correspondence study, teleconferences, and other mechanisms for distance learning.

Issues of Quality and Credibility

Regardless of where and how courses are offered, the most important factor contributing to quality and credibility in certificate programs is high-quality instruction. As in traditional degree programs, the quality of instruction depends on the quality of the faculty who teach in the programs. Certificate courses are generally taught by permanent or adjunct faculty at the institution, or by other practicing professionals who satisfy standards established by academic officers and related faculty at these institutions.

Although certificate programs can be administered by academic units, they are most often managed by general extension and continuing education divisions when such units exist at the institution. On some campuses, all certificate programs are centralized in a single operation, while on others different academic units simultaneously provide programs. The organization and management of certificate programs are always subject to institutional policies and procedures of operation that are distinct from more traditional degree programs. Question-and-answer sessions with certificate program planners and developers at national conferences suggest that certificate programs are most intensely scrutinized when introduced in the more traditional academic bureaucracies. Although in my computer search of the literature for this book, I found no studies that might explain specific instances of flourishing and of floundering of these programs, most instances of development of and experimentation with these formats appear to be occurring in settings where administrators are encouraged and feel free to respond to immediate societal and technological demands. Certainly, the issue of institutional receptivity to certificate programs is worthy of further investigation (see Walshok, this volume; Snider, Marasco, and Keene, this volume).

However unreceptive some colleges and universities may be to certificate programs, the range of public and private accredited institutions offering these programs in the United States is impressive. Certificate programs exist in many types of academic institutions: liberal arts, church affiliated, research oriented, vocational-technical schools, land grant universities, to name but a few. Neither type nor size of institutions appears to predict whether or not certificate programs are available. Smaller and medium-sized colleges and universities are as likely as their larger public and private counterparts to provide these types of programs. The salient factor seems to be institutional recognition that an alternative credential to academic degrees is needed to respond to changes in the educational geography of an increasingly learning-oriented society.

Conclusion

Certificate programs are concentrated studies developed most often for career enhancement and personal enrichment. Many are conceived as a result of increasing specialization of careers and individual and professional needs for additional job skills, updating, and expanded work opportunities. Although these programs present traditional educational institutions with new challenges, creative and innovative organizations are impressively responding in their development of contemporary curricula for evolving and emerging fields.

References

Carpenter, J. *Completions in Institutions of Higher Education, 1986–87.* National Center for Education Statistics Report no. 90–322. Washington, D.C.: U.S. Department of Education, Office of Educational Research and Improvement, 1989.

Gilley, J. W., and Gailbraith, M. W. "Professionalization and Professional Certification." In University of Wyoming, *Adult Education Research 28th Annual Conference Proceedings.* Laramie: University of Wyoming, 1987.

Gonnella, J. S., and Zeleznik, C. "Strengthening the Relations Between Professional Education and Performance." In S. M. Grabowski (ed.), *Strengthening Connections Between Education and Performance.* New Directions for Adult and Continuing Education, no. 18. San Francisco: Jossey-Bass, 1983.

Gordon, J. D. "An Experimental Course in Elements of Digital Computer Technology for the Training of Computer Programmers." *Dissertation Abstracts International,* 1987, *48,* 01A.

Hankin, J. H. "Where Were You Twelve Years Ago?" *Vital Speeches of the Day,* 1988, *54* (10), 300–306.

Lopos, G. J., Holt, M. E., Bohlander, R. E., and Wells, J. H. (eds.). *Peterson's Guide to Certificate Programs at American Colleges and Universities.* Princeton, N.J.: Peterson's Guides, 1988.

Phillips, L. W. "Thoughts on Improving Mandatory Continuing Education." *Lifelong Learning Forum,* 1987, *4* (2), 1, 5–6.

Smith, A. O. "The Relationship of Age, Sex, Education, Experience, Income, and Field of Preparation to Job Satisfaction of University Career Certificate Graduates." Unpublished doctoral dissertation, School of Education and Human Development, George Washington University, 1987.

Margaret E. Holt is associate professor of adult education at the University of Georgia, Athens, and she is an associate with the Charles F. Kettering Foundation in Dayton, Ohio.

Using information from the fields of instructional design and technology, educational psychology, training, and evaluation, this chapter presents heuristics that can be applied to certificate programs.

Heuristics for Planning and Presenting Effective Certificate Programs

Barry D. Bratton

The content and perspectives presented in this chapter may be different, even debatable, to some readers, particularly those steeped in the tenets of adult education. Instructional design is a relatively new field in education. It advocates that the teacher (an expert in a field) is responsible for systematically planning the goals, objectives, instructional activities, and evaluation of educational programs. This field also promotes the use of mastery learning and criterion-referenced testing. Readers who are not familiar with the instructional design field may find the references listed at the end of the chapter helpful.

Certificate programs come in all sizes, address myriad topics, involve a spectrum of learners, and generate revenue for sponsoring institutions. Once a cottage industry, these programs are now enjoying unprecedented growth. With this visibility comes the responsibility to provide the best educational programs possible. Using information from the fields of instructional design and technology, educational psychology, training, and evaluation, this chapter presents heuristics that can be applied to certificate programs. Specifically, I describe an instructional design model that has been developed to guide teachers when they are preparing instructional programs.

Typically, when teachers plan courses or programs, they think first

I acknowledge the help provided by Shelly Bartensteine, director of certificate programs, Office of Extended Education, California State University, Fullerton, and George Lopos, associate dean, Continuing Education, The University of Iowa, in the preparation of this chapter.

about how many hours must be filled, the number of students, the topics to be presented, the textbooks, the assignments, and the tests. Then they prepare syllabi to convey this information to the learners. At the first meetings of their classes, they distribute the syllabi, give brief overviews of the courses, and point out the deadlines for papers, projects, and examinations. They then are likely to launch into a series of prepared lectures (or lectures-discussions) on specific topics. Occasionally, an instructor is successful at igniting a class discussion, but most of the time the students are focused on taking correct notes from the lecture. If this characterization of teacher and learner activities is valid, certificate program administrators and instructors may wish to investigate alternatives for planning and providing quality instruction.

The field of instructional design and technology is a relatively new specialization in the areas of education and training. It is a hybrid field, for its roots can be traced to a variety of disciplines such as educational psychology, instructional psychology, educational communications, training, testing, and curriculum development. As a discipline, it offers unique perspectives for the planning, delivery, and evaluation of programs. Today, scholars and practitioners in this field are focusing on ways to apply knowledge to the teaching-learning process and are researching promising models that will eventually help us predict what works most effectively to produce high-quality instruction (Briggs, Gustafson, and Tillman, 1991).

The purpose of this chapter is to present information about the field of instructional design and technology and to suggest how it might enhance certificate programs in particular. I pursue these ends by describing a prominent instructional design model that is often cited in the literature. There are many excellent textbooks on the market that provide guidance for designing instructional and training programs. Several of the more prominent ones are listed in the reference section of this chapter. For the purposes of this chapter, I use the approach advocated by Jerrold Kemp. Not only is his model widely accepted by experts in the field, but his book enjoys acceptance in educational institutions and training organizations in many countries.

The Kemp Model of Instructional Design

Jerrold Kemp's (1985) book *The Instructional Design Process* describes a model for designing instruction in any discipline. His nearly thirty years of experience in consulting with classroom instructors at all levels of education convinced him that teachers do not plan, teach, and evaluate in identical ways. He noted that some teachers are very systematic, while others prefer a holistic approach. Some think first about the content, others about the students, and still others about the teaching methods. However, based on his extensive teaching experience and observations of excellent teachers, he became aware that all effective teachers similarly take a number of factors into consideration as they plan their instruction. Figure 2.1 presents his characterization of these factors. Observe that the model contains thirteen components.

According to the Kemp model, teachers and trainers should consider each of these components as they plan their instruction. Note that this model is systemic in nature. The author does not prescribe a set procedure for considering the thirteen elements; however, it is important that each element in the model be considered by the teacher at some point—sometimes at several points—during the planning process. The graphic in Figure 2.1 reminds us to attend to all thirteen components of the model as the instructional plan evolves and to ensure that all the elements are interrelated.

Learning Needs. This component refers to the necessity or purpose of the instruction. "Needs" in this case means a deficit in the learner's knowledge, skill, or attitude. Needs can be identified by surveys, interviews, tests, and observations of performance. Needs should not be confused with "wants," such as "I need (want) a course in stargazing." Think of a learning need as a discrepancy between what a student knows at the start of a course and what he or she should know at the end. The gap between the present level of knowledge and the desired level is called an *instructional need.*

Suggestion: An instructional program should not be designed unless a verified learning need exists. Otherwise, the instructor's time and the time and money of students are wasted.

Figure 2.1. Kemp Instructional Design Model (1985)

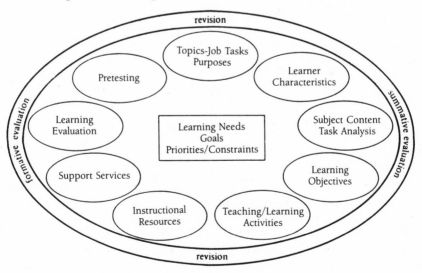

Source: The Instructional Design Process by Jerrold Kemp. Copyright © 1985 by Harper & Row Publishers, Inc. Reprinted by permission of HarperCollins Publishers.

Topics, Job Tasks, and Purposes. This component refers to the main areas of content or skills that will be presented during the instruction/training. This information should be consistent with the results of the learning needs assessment.

Suggestion: While textbooks and the instructor's experiences contribute to the course content, the learners—particularly adults—should be invited to identify the content and skills that they want to learn in the course.

Learner Characteristics. This component refers to the general information gathered about the learners before the formal instruction/training commences. In many cases, data regarding their previous education, areas of expertise, current and prior work experiences, motives for seeking more education, preferred learning styles, and so on can help in the planning of class activities and assignments.

Suggestion: Survey the students before the course begins or distribute a questionnaire at the first class meeting, asking for background information that may be helpful to the course instruction.

Subject Content and Task Analysis. This component refers to the process of determining the specific information, skills, and beliefs that will be presented. Subject content analysis means deciding what facts, concepts, and principles will be presented about a body of information and their order of introduction in the course. Task analysis is the process of uncovering all of the steps (physical or mental) required to complete a task. Experts who teach may have internalized their fields to such a high degree that when teaching, they forget to explain all of the details of the subject and unknowingly link one concept to another without providing a rationale to the students. Frequently, they use jargon that is unfamiliar to students. A careful analysis of the content to be presented to students will help them grasp the essential information.

Suggestion: Analyze carefully the content that will be taught so that all essential terms, concepts, and principles, as well as the details and linkages, are included.

Pretest the Learners. This component refers to the course-specific information gathered about the learners at the beginning of the program. The purpose for the teacher is to learn how much the learners already know about the course content to be taught and if the learners have all of the prerequisite knowledge and skills for the course. Armed with this information profile, the teacher can start the instruction at a level that is appropriate for the majority of the learners.

Suggestion: Whenever possible, require the learners to complete a questionnaire before the course starts or at the first meeting. Some questions should inquire about knowledge that is essential background information for the course and that all learners should have already acquired. Other questions should focus on topics that will be discussed during the course and with which students need not be familiar. The answers to these questions can provide a profile of the learners' current knowledge and thus help the instructor further determine course topics and activities.

Learning Objectives. This component refers to what the instructor wants the students to learn as a result of the instruction. Some instructors do not believe that it is appropriate to tell students what they are expected to learn. They believe that good students will achieve the intended learning objectives, while poor students are doomed to fail. The instructional design field advocates the practice of informing learners about what they are expected to learn and how they will be evaluated. Objectives necessarily fall into three generally accepted learning domains: cognitive, affective, and psychomotor. Cognitive objectives are helpful when the intent is to teach facts, concepts, and principles. Affective objectives promote the acquisition of new attitudes. Psychomotor objectives are used to describe physical movement.

Suggestion: Inform the learners at the beginning of the program about what they are expected to learn by the end of the program and how their learning will be assessed.

Teaching and Learning Activities. This component refers to the activities that the instructor plans to pursue during the course. Just as we would expect an expert pilot to be able to fly more than one type of aircraft and a physician to provide more than one type of prescription to patients, a good instructor should know about and be able to use a variety of instructional methods with students. For example, an effective instructor is able to deliver lectures, lead discussion groups, provide individualized assistance, present case studies, select and operate audiovisual programs, and create individualized self-instructional modules.

Suggestions: Inform the learners at the beginning of the program that a variety of activities will be used. If necessary, students who are not familiar with a particular method should be taught its fundamental premises and techniques. An "impaired instructor" who is not familiar with a variety of instructional strategies should seek information and training on them.

Instructional Resources. This component refers to the task of keeping abreast of potential teaching resources and acquiring the competence to judge their potential effectiveness and to use them properly. Resources are anything that can help the instructor teach more effectively and efficiently. They can include guest speakers, case studies, simulations, charts, graphs, photographs, audio recordings, videotapes, slides, films, overhead transparencies, computer programs, and interactive-video programs.

Suggestion: Become adept and comfortable at using all types of instructional materials and audiovisual devices. Keep abreast of computer-based training programs.

Support Services. This component refers to the sources for the instructional aids mentioned above. Examples include audiovisual centers, libraries, museums, technology centers, civic groups, training companies, textbook publishers, and colleagues.

Suggestion: Become familiar with and form a network of sources and contacts for potential instructional aids.

Learning Evaluation. This component refers to assessments of the degree to which each learner acquires the knowledge, skills, and beliefs specified in the instructional objectives. Questions used to evaluate the students should be related to the instructional objectives. If the program is based on the mastery learning philosophy, it is essential that questions be drawn directly from the learning objectives. On the other hand, if the norm-based approach (grading on a curve) is used, create questions that produce a bell-shaped curve with the best students getting the highest grades and the poorest students the lowest. Be familiar with the guidelines for preparing valid and reliable evaluative tests such as multiple choice, true-false, matching, short answer, checklists, and rating scales.

Suggestions: Tell students how they will be evaluated during and at the end of the course. Use the learning objectives and the content topics as guides when preparing test questions and assigning projects. Use norm-based testing, mastery testing, or some combination of the two. Inform the students at the first class meeting about the testing philosophy and methods to be employed.

Formative Evaluation. This component refers to feedback gathered throughout the course for the purpose of making improvements. The task of monitoring how well the students are achieving the learning objectives during the instruction can be accomplished by quizzes, class activities, written assignments, projects, informal talks with the students, and so on. To monitor the effectiveness of the course, the teacher periodically can ask the students for their perceptions and suggestions for making it more effective and interesting.

Suggestion: If the learners are not acquiring the subject matter, discuss the problem with them and make modifications in the teaching-learning activities and evaluation procedures. By carefully monitoring what is happening during the course, the teacher can detect if a problem is caused by the learners' lack of preparation or by his or her own faulty assumptions about the learners' backgrounds or levels of self-confidence.

Summative Evaluation. This component refers to evaluation of the course in retrospect for the purpose of improving it for the next presentation. Another aim is to be able to provide evidence to the sponsor that the program is successful in terms of both effectiveness and efficiency. Effectiveness refers to the number of learners who reached an acceptable level of achievement for each objective. Factors that influence the effectiveness of a course include learner characteristics such as pretest and prerequisite knowledge, the difficulty level of the content, the teaching-learning activities employed, and the quality of the formative and summative evaluation systems. A course that produces superior learning levels within a short period of time is labeled both effective and efficient. Efficiency is defined in terms of cost and time. Costs are frequently related to the time needed to develop and present the course.

Suggestion: Calculate the costs and the benefits of each course. The instructional costs may include such factors as facilities, materials, instructor(s), support personnel, hardware and software, overhead charges, and repairs. The benefits of a course can be documented in terms of number of students who completed the course, amount learned, and student evaluations.

Revision. This component refers to the process of reflecting on how well a course was taught for the purpose of future improvement. The review may include the various types of tests (needs assessment, pretest, prerequisite test, posttest) that were employed. There may be a review to update the content or to determine the instructor who will be in charge of the course in the future.

Suggestions: Schedule a review meeting soon after the course is ended. Involve all of the persons who contributed to it. Appoint someone to take notes so that future instructors can benefit from the discussion. Keep the course design, all of the accompanying materials, and the meeting notes in a secure location so that other instructors can benefit from these materials. In this chapter, I have focused on but one type of instructional design model that helps teachers prepare, present, and evaluate their certificate courses. There are other viewpoints and models that may be helpful to instructors of certificate programs.

Sample Applications of Kemp's Model

Two illustrations of the application of instructional design principles are provided in Exhibits 2.1 and 2.2. In both cases, note the orderly progression of the teaching and learning activities to motivate and assist the students to achieve the course objectives. Exhibit 2.1 is a design for a course in the health sciences. Note how the plan follows the Kemp model. With this design plan, different instructors can present the course knowing that all the participants will receive the same quality experience. If (when) the course is revised, it is suggested that all of the instructors participate in the redesign.

Exhibit 2.2 is a partial design for a certificate course in transportation demand management. It includes the need and goals of the course, the kinds of individuals who will likely benefit from it, the major topics covered, the overall learner objectives, and a plan for the first meeting of the course.

Summary

Effective classroom educators know that teaching is a complex process. Unfortunately, many have not received practical training in the methodology

Exhibit 2.1. Sample Design of Instructional Unit in the Health Sciences: Technique for Washing Hands for Medical Asepsis

General Purposes
1. To learn the correct techniques for washing hands
2. To understand the reasons for maintaining an aseptic environment in medical settings

Learner Characteristics
1. Twenty first-year health science students majoring in laboratory technology
2. High level of motivation
3. One-fourth of the students have observed other health professionals using hand-washing techniques

Preassessment
1. Is it possible that patients can catch diseases from people who work in a hospital? (prerequisite question)
2. Is it essential to wash your hands after contacting a patient? (pretest question)
3. Name three ways by which bacteria can be transmitted in a hospital (pretest question)
4. List the steps in correctly washing one's hands (pretest question)

Learning Objectives
1. Explain why aseptic conditions must be maintained at all times
2. Name the routes by which bacteria can be transmitted in a health care facility
3. Describe circumstances that necessitate hand washing
4. Demonstrate proper hand-washing techniques

Note: So far the instructor has informed the learners of the goal of the course, administered a pretest to determine how much the learners know about aseptic procedures, inquired about the demographics of the class, and informed the students of the learning objectives they will master.

Subject Content
1. Definition of "aseptic":
    a. Levels of infection-free conditions and their potential consequences
    b. Implications for health workers, patients, and patients' families
2. Routes by which bacteria can be transmitted:
    a. Patient to patient
    b. Employee to patient
    c. Patient to employee
    d. Employee to employee
    e. Hospital equipment to patient or employee
3. Situations in which hand washing is required:
    a. Before and after contact with a patient
    b. After contact with waste or contaminated materials
    c. Before handling food or food receptacles
    d. Any time your hands become soiled
4. Technique for aseptic hand washing:
    a. Turn water on to warm setting
    b. Wet hands
    c. Apply soap thoroughly on palms and backs of hands and between fingers and under nails
    d. Wash hands with ten strong movements

Exhibit 2.1 *(continued)*

e. Wash fingers and spaces between them with ten strong strokes
f. Wash wrists and up to three inches above the wrists
g. Repeat steps c–f
h. Rinse thoroughly with the final rinse falling from the wrist to the fingers
i. Use a towel to turn off the water and discard the towel

Note: The instructor gathered the above information from professional experience, from existing documentation, and from observing an expert perform the sequence.

Teacher-Student Activities

1. Teacher welcomes students to the class in medical asepsis; distributes a handout containing the learning objectives, the planned activities, and the evaluation methods; encourages questions; students listen and ask questions
2. Teacher gives a brief lecture/discussion on the need for aseptic conditions in health care facilities; students take notes and ask questions
3. Teacher asks students to watch a videotape on hand-washing procedures and to note when they observe that improper procedures are used; students watch and take notes
4. Teacher asks students to form groups of three to compare their notes; teacher moves around the room monitoring the discussions and responding to questions
5. Teacher asks one group to present their list to the class while other groups listen and compare lists; teacher summarizes the improper procedures and shows the correct methods
6. Teacher assigns students to read two sections in the laboratory manual describing the correct procedures for hand washing; students read the two manual sections
7. Teacher assigns students to view a second videotape demonstrating the correct procedures for hand washing and to bring questions to the next class; students view the videotape and ask questions
8. Teacher responds to the students' notes and comments from the videotape; demonstrates proper aseptic procedures as the students watch; observes as students practice and gives feedback; students practice and give each other feedback
9. Teacher shows a third video that contains more difficult cases; students watch the videotape and discriminate proper from improper procedures
10. With a preceptor observing, each student draws blood from another student; teacher and "student/patient" give feedback
11. Teacher continues to give corrections and feedback until all students master the technique
12. Teacher holds an open discussion with the students to answer any questions and concerns

Support Services

1. Personnel: one content expert to provide essential knowledge and skills; two laboratory technicians to supervise the skill-building exercises
2. Facilities: learning laboratory with sinks, towels, and soap; access to patients
3. Videotape: rent, purchase, or produce a quality instructional videotape on this topic

Note: The instructor planned many opportunities for students to practice the skill in simulated and live situations.

Exhibit 2.1 *(continued)*

Learning Evaluation

1. Why are aseptic conditions required in a hospital?
2. Name the routes by which bacteria can be transmitted in a hospital
3. Watch a new videotape on hand washing and write a report on its thoroughness
4. Perform a proper hand-washing procedure

Formative Evaluation of the Unit

1. Compare the level of learning achieved by each student in this unit to students in previous units
2. Compare the amount of time and the number of personnel required to complete this unit to those of prior units

Summative Evaluation of the Unit

1. Do the learners retain and use their knowledge, skills, and attitudes over a long period of time?
2. Does the cost of the new instruction remain at a reasonable level?
3. Can the unit be updated easily if new techniques and knowledge emerge?

Note: The instructor evaluated the course in several ways: by testing the students' knowledge for the purpose of assigning grades, for comparing the effects of new design to previous classes, and for learning how the course might be improved in the future. If the decision is made to modify the course, the data from the learning evaluations and the results of the formative and summative evaluations will provide clues for making changes in the unit.

Exhibit 2.2. Sample Partial Design for a Certificate Course in Transportation

Course Title

Certificate Award in Transportation Demand Management (TDM)

Course Status

A noncredit certificate award in TDM

Need

Legislators and environmental regulators across the country are drafting new requirements, implementing stronger controls on auto emissions, and introducing life-style changes to reduce the number of cars on freeways. Company-mandated employee ride-share programs are one example. Other programs are being developed that also will influence both public and private businesses. Individuals who have an interest or training in the field of land use, environmental planning, or public administration need to expand their knowledge bases to include the specialized skills associated with designing, implementing, maintaining, and evaluating TDM programs. The consequences of not producing feasible plans can be costly to employers.

Goal

This course will help participants gain an understanding of the TDM concept, comply with current and future regulations, and plan effective TDM programs.

Exhibit 2.2 *(continued)*

Learner Characteristics

Persons with backgrounds in one or more of the following areas will be most successful in this course: certified employee transportation coordinators, transportation coordinators, government employees, transportation consultants, environmental planners, paralegals, administrative assistants, clerical employees, and governmental legislative and policy employees.

Subject Content

The relationships among air quality, mobility, and land use are examined, as well as the impact of the regulatory setting on these three areas. Approximately 60 percent of the content will focus on specific TDM techniques and on the design and implementation of effective TDM programs.

Learning Objectives of the Course

1. Describe the relationships among mobility, air quality, and land use
2. Define key regulatory schemes for land use, mobility, and air quality, including the Air Quality Management Plan, the Congestion Management Plan, and the Regional Mobility Plan
3. Explain the roles and relationships of key agencies and participants related to air quality, mobility, and land use
4. Recall key TDM principles
5. Identify resources that enable participants to stay current with regulatory trends
6. Apply TDM principles and methods to the design of a TDM program
7. Review and determine the adequacy of a traffic mitigation plan
8. Solve case problems related to various business situations
9. Produce a TDM plan.

The learning objectives for the first class meeting are (1) to learn the state and national laws that are affected by TDM implementation, and (2) to be able to discuss some of the legal and environmental issues related to implementing TDM.

Plan for Teaching and Learning Activities at the First Meeting of the Course

Teacher	Learners
1. Welcome learners to the course; ask them to watch a videotape (*Race to Save the Planet*) and then facilitate the discussion by asking questions and offering counterscenarios	1. Watch the videotape, discuss the content, express opinions, and ask questions
2. Ask the learners to introduce themselves and their reasons for taking the course; instructor introduces self	2. Introductions
3. Distribute a survey asking for the name, work experience, education, career goals, and reason for taking this course	3. Complete survey
4. Distribute the course syllabus with the nine course objectives and the objectives for each class meeting, discuss project assignments and class logistics, and encourage questions	4. Read syllabus and ask questions

Exhibit 2.2 (*continued*)

Teacher	Learners
5. Present an overview lecture using handouts and overhead transparencies on APC Agencies, federal and state laws, and SIPS, APCD, and TDM incentives; encourage questions and discussion at any time	5. Listen, take notes, and ask questions
6. Form small groups to discuss and summarize the main points of the lecture and their implications	6. Discuss, summarize, and ask questions
7. Ask two groups to report on their discussion points	7. Listen to the reports and give reactions and alternative perspectives
8. Summarize the main ideas	8. Listen and take notes

Note: At this point the instructor feels that the learners have grasped the major points and are ready to use their knowledge in the following debate exercise.

9. Introduce a debate: "Build It Versus Manage It"; describe the purpose of the exercise, choose debaters and observers/participants, give each debater a role to play during the exercise, and tell remainder of class to note the main points from each side of the debate	9. Listen and take notes

of instructional design. Frequently, they are told what effective instruction means but not trained in how to do it. The Kemp model is one of several excellent models; others are listed in the reference section. Judicious application of these models will likely enhance your teaching and the quality of instruction received by your students, whether in certificate programs or in traditional classes. The two examples drawn from actual certificate programs should help the reader see how the more general principles of instructional design and some of Kemp's model are applied to realistic learning situations.

References

Briggs, L., Gustafson, K., Tillman, M. (eds.). *Instructional Design: Principles and Applications.* Englewood Cliffs, N.J.: Educational Technology, 1991.

Kemp, J. *The Instructional Design Process.* New York: Harper & Row, 1985.

Barry D. Bratton is associate professor and head of the Instructional Design and Technology Program, College of Education, University of Iowa.

Certificate programs are playing an increasingly significant role in higher education, representing unique educational experiences for adult learners. A collaborative approach to program design, marketing, instruction, and evaluation can yield high-quality interdisciplinary programs that effectively serve educational needs.

Evaluation and Quality Control in Certificate Programs

Mary Lindenstein Walshok

The value of quality is central in higher education in general and in continuing higher education in particular. Its special significance to the practice of continuing higher education derives from the complex task of providing educational programs that unite the needs of practitioners in the workplace with the educational resources of conventional academics and experts. Most certificate programs accomplish that task.

Assurance of quality is intimately tied to recognition of the fact that perceptions of quality differ according to one's relationship to the educational program and its outcomes. For those with the responsibility of creating the knowledge base, that is, researchers and scholars, quality is measured by empirical indicators adduced through evaluation and research. For those interested in using or applying the knowledge, for example, practitioners and employers, quality may be measured with factors such as relevance to workplace requirements. And for those attempting to master the knowledge and skills, that is, students, quality may be measured by yet other factors such as assistance in getting a job.

As organized sequences of study that do not result in degrees, certificate programs face numerous problems. Because, more often than not, a certificate program, whether designed for continuing education or traditional credit, is an alternative to or a step beyond the substance of traditional degree programs, it is designed to serve educational purposes different from those served by degree programs. Nonetheless, the standards of quality applied to certificate programs are often tied to the purposes and expectations of degree programs. Degree programs in most colleges and universities are designed by faculty committees, reviewed and endorsed by academic senates, and ultimately approved by state and related higher education accrediting bodies that adhere to a broadly agreed upon set of bureaucratic standards. They also involve more courses and longer periods of study than are required by certificate programs. The latter are usually more narrow in their educational purposes, although more broad in terms of the range of expertise on which they rely in their design, endorsement, and implementation. They transmit knowledge and skills in a shorter time frame, with fewer course requirements.

In light of these differences in educational purposes, the process of assuring and evaluating quality in certificate programs must be based on principles different from those applied to most degree programs. The process, from the beginning, must be collaborative and it must result in academic programs whose design, implementation, and review include knowledge experts, experienced practitioners, and students in the program.

The quality-assurance problem is further complicated by the fact that certificates can be of at least three types. One type involves basic introductions to established fields of study or practice. These fields frequently have long traditions and thus there is widespread consensus about the core knowledge base of each and the necessary tools of practice. Examples are paralegal studies and introductions to microcomputer engineering. A second type involves updates of existing fields. These certificate programs bring the student or practitioner in contact with recent developments or cutting-edge ideas, for example, developments in securities regulation and new treatment modalities or therapies for medical practitioners. The third type involves interdisciplinary or emerging fields. For these certificate programs, there is much less consensus about what represents core knowledge or essential skills. An emerging field such as toxics and hazardous waste management or an interdisciplinary area such as international business are examples. With the exception of the first type of certificate, which introduces a student to a basic area of knowledge, using a short format, it is difficult to imagine how quality can be assured without relying on a variety of resources in addition to faculty experts. These results could include practitioners, employers, interested skilled people, policymakers or regulators, and even journalists with specialties in a particular field.

In this chapter, I introduce a way of thinking more broadly about the resources that a program planner can utilize to assure quality in certificate programs. These resources are essential at the design, implementation, and program evaluation stages. At each stage, quality assurance rests on how well a program planner incorporates the following: (1) a core knowledge base that is accurate, timely, and relevant, (2) input from program beneficiaries, (3) appropriate methodology and pedagogy for the type of knowledge and skills being developed, (4) recruitment, training, and review of appropriate instructional staff, (5) measurement of the learning gains of participants, and (6) regular updates of program content and methodology.

What follows is a series of issues that a planner should bear in mind in order to facilitate the development of a certificate program. Together, consideration of the issues can contribute significantly to a program whose quality is recognized and validated by a diverse group of stakeholders: university faculty, off-campus practitioners, and adult learners.

The ideas presented here on quality assurance are based on my "hands-on" experience of program development in the context of a major research university. The University of California has one of the most extensive programs of continuing professional education in the United States, serving 400,000 enrollees annually in noncredit programs for which no state budgetary support is received. The university's certificate programs are nonetheless subject to on-campus faculty review and approval, as well as to "marketplace" endorsement. I have also found Robinson's (1991) guide to the development of certificate programs to be a valuable source of information and ideas. What follows are a series of issues a planner should bear in mind while facilitating the development of certificate programs. Together they should contribute significantly to a program whose quality is recognized and validated by a diverse group of stakeholders: university faculty, off-campus practitioners, and adult learners.

Ensuring the Quality of Core Knowledge

In a university setting, the quality and integrity of knowledge are usually tied to the reputation and credentials of the person developing or transmitting that knowledge. Research universities in particular have elaborate and exhaustive techniques for assessing faculty quality. These range from output measures such as where one publishes and by whom work is reviewed, to impact measures such as the number of reviews and commentaries on a given work and the frequency with which ideas or data are footnoted, to reputation measures such as peer review of work, student evaluations of teaching, and extent and type of consulting and community service. It is essential that the resources on which a planner relies in identifying the core knowledge or substance of a proposed certificate program bear equivalent "markers" of quality.

A planner may rely on only one individual or on a small number of "experts" when defining the intellectual parameters of a program, but each source should have superb credentials that are recognizable and verifiable in a variety of contexts. For example, when the task is to design a management certificate, exclusive reliance on a management professor with primarily academic publications, little consulting experience, and no hands-on business experience can be as ill-advised as exclusive reliance on a professional manager with limited formal education and little professional reputation or involvement outside his or her own company. Rarely do we find an individual whose knowledge and reputation are equally sound in academia and in the world of practice, so the use of a mix of individuals who are regarded as "solid" in their fields can achieve early, substantive input on program design that is both comprehensive and accurate. In other words, either choose experts for planning committees who together represent a variety of contexts—knowledge generation and research, hands-on practice, classroom effectiveness—*or* find an individual whose reputation is strong and credentials respected in a variety of contexts. In my own institution, the designs of certificates in such diverse fields as alcohol counseling, marketing, urban planning, and teaching English as a second language have drawn on the expertise of carefully selected advisory committees composed of people with superb reputations and credentials. In selecting such persons, it is important to take the time to research their backgrounds and to meet with them personally.

Ensuring Input from Program Beneficiaries

This step is integrally related to the points in the preceding section. It is essential that practitioners and users of the knowledge be included in the planning and implementation process, for they possess the kind of expertise that, combined with basic content knowledge, is critical to the development of a qualitatively appropriate curriculum. The raison d'etre of a certificate program is as often dictated by a need in a community or industry as it is by the employment contingencies of individuals.

The management of toxic and hazardous waste, for example, represents a need that institutions of all types—public schools, hospitals, industrial sites, real estate developments—are confronting. Based on this need, there is a strong social demand for a type of expertise and practitioner that has not existed before. The design of a program developed to train these new practitioners needs to reflect not only what chemists and health practitioners know about toxic and hazardous waste but also what needs must be met in the workplaces and institutional sites of waste management. Employers need people with new types of expertise, and those seeking to develop that expertise need to be prepared for the real-world challenges that they will face. There is at present no established college curriculum on the topic of waste management, so faculty must work collaboratively with the beneficiaries of a certificate program to ensure appropriate content and to arrive at a shared definition of quality.

The involvement of beneficiaries, institutional and individual, in the design of a certificate program affects more than just program content. Practitioners can often identify credible instructors and sources of expertise in the field. They can give valuable input on the timing, sequencing, and method of delivery for various components of the program, as well as on the most opportune time of day and location for the program courses. And they can suggest ways of "framing," promoting, and publicizing the program to facilitate adequate enrollment numbers. Overall, the quality and success of a certificate program can be greatly enhanced by the participation, at the earliest stages, of practitioners and institutional beneficiaries.

Ensuring Appropriate Methodology

A well-crafted advisory committee made up of persons with diverse expertise and interests can also contribute to quality by ensuring that the knowledge and skills transmitted through the program are delivered in an appropriate pedagogical manner. The reliance in degree programs on the expert lecturer at the front of the class transmitting his or her wisdom to an unknowing student body violates a number of assumptions underlying certificate programs, especially those emphasizing interdisciplinary knowledge. In certificate programs, the interaction is often with students who possess a great deal of expertise not possessed by the instructor and who are, in a real sense, peers. Often, the knowledge transmitted is highly interdisciplinary; problem solving is often an important educational objective, and the highly motivated adult learner is capable of a great deal of independent work. For all these reasons the program planner needs to be both flexible when thinking about program input and versatile in approaches to instruction. Simulation exercises, case studies, and field research may be valuable. Team learning through shared projects as well as team teaching may be appropriate. Self-paced components, electronic mail, and seminar networks among students are all ways to enhance learning and ensure quality. But they need to be part of the program design from the outset. At my own university, executive education is not based on courses and an accumulation of units but rather on an integrated series of modules involving such diverse elements as conventional lectures by university faculty, team projects, interactions with chief executive officers, library research, and computer networking among busy working adults.

Quality is enhanced by appropriate delivery and how knowledge gets shared and transmitted. Certificate programs should not mirror the narrow concepts of pedagogy still prevalent in the conventional professor-student relationship. Indeed, the involvement of practitioners in program planning often results in access to learning sites, significant individuals, and pedagogically useful equipment not within the reach of on-campus faculty. Thus, limited on-campus resources do not constitute a barrier to quality learning experiences when the program planner relies on a wide circle of individual and institutional input when putting together a certificate program.

Recruiting Appropriate Instructors

In any good business, as in any good college or university, people are everything, and the quality of the people involved is often what differentiates one institution from another, one academic program from another. In the increasingly competitive marketplace of continuing higher education, the skills, reputation, and integrity of the people associated with a given program may be one of its most critical characteristics. Quality people—on advisory committees, in instructional roles, and as guest lecturers and program mentors—draw quality students. The ability to draw high-quality students, students who are motivated, knowledgeable, and well positioned in their organizations, is one way that people judge the quality of a certificate program, and the higher the quality of the faculty and program leaders, the greater the likelihood of high-quality students.

The world of noncredit and professional continuing education is highly vulnerable to self-promoting instructors who are trying to build careers or personal businesses or who have not established credibility in institutional settings or professional roles. The same care involved in researching the credentials, reputation, and integrity of planning and advisory committee members must be exercised in the recruitment of instructional staff for certificate programs. Whether the program needs a faculty member or hands-on practitioner, my advice is to go for the "hard to get" rather than the easily available. Go for the person who sees teaching in the program as an opportunity to engage new ideas, students, or constituencies rather than an occasion to make a few extra dollars. Go for the person with a reputation for leadership in his or her area of expertise rather than someone who teaches from a textbook. Go for the person who is so well connected that he or she will be seen by students as truly knowledgeable about what is going on in a field and will be valued as a potential resource long after the program is completed.

Whether a college is in a small town or a big city, is a local or a national institution, or has a reputation for good teaching or for innovative research, it is possible to recruit high-quality faculty. But the program planner must be proactive and capable of judging integrity and quality in others and using the suggestions and leads provided by advisers. In my own institution, we stress depth of content expertise in our continuing educators because their primary responsibility is to make important content judgments and recruit credible advisory committees and program faculty. If the programmer is a generalist, it is imperative that he or she build strong advisory groups to help in these detail-oriented decisions. Any acceptance of instructors without close examination of their credentials and reputations runs significant qualitative risks.

Once credible instructors have been found, time must be spent one-on-one or in groups on orienting them to the overall objectives of the certificate program, highlighting content areas and the rationale for the pace, timing and sequencing of given content areas, and helping them see where they "fit" in the overall program. Principles of adult education can be useful in this orientation, but continuing educators need to resist overemphasis on the problems of the adult learner at the expense of the content and pedagogical issues surrounding what is to be learned. A quality program must address both of these areas of concern.

Measuring Learning Gains

Universities are struggling with the question of how to measure the effects of their educational programs on undergraduates and graduates. Thus, it is not surprising that this is a difficult issue for continuing education as well. Nonetheless, there are ways to assess whether a certificate program is accomplishing its objectives and making a difference in the lives of the students who are supposedly using the knowledge, and in the community or institution that is supposedly benefiting from the real-world applications of that knowledge. In fact, the focused objectives of many certificate programs and the clear identity of the multiple stakeholders in a given program make review and evaluation somewhat easier than is possible in the dispersed and uncertain worlds entered by graduates of our institutions of higher learning.

At the University of California-Extension, frequent and regular course evaluations are administered to students in all of the continuing education efforts. Evaluations represent a way to assess student motivations for taking the course, satisfaction with the content and instruction, and learning gains and content relevance to personal objectives. In general, with personal computers, any programmer can efficiently ensure that evaluations are designed, administered, tallied, and given to instructors for feedback.

A second simple way to assess program effectiveness, particularly in the nondegree realm of certificate programs, is to examine the rates of reenrollment by previous students and first-time enrollments by new students based on program reputation and word of mouth. These rates, taken alone, are not measures of quality but in combination with evaluations and other assessment methods can provide insight into program effectiveness.

Follow-up interviews with program graduates, either by phone or in specially scheduled focus groups, can also serve as valuable evaluation tools. My institution is increasingly hiring full-time students to do scripted telephone interviews both for marketing and for specific program evaluation purposes. Follow-up interviews with employers and institutions putatively served by certificate programs are also highly desirable. When done in person by program directors, they can yield a wealth of information and good will. Telephone interviews and focus group interviews are also effective tools. Mailed surveys can also be used, but judiciously as response rates vary considerably. For programs in which students have invested a great deal of time, such as certificate programs, the return rates are likely to be better than are typically achieved with general surveys. Twenty well-placed telephone interviews, however, can yield more substance and detail than are garnered through a written questionnaire returned by fifty people.

Finally, a reliable indicator of success and quality is the amount of "repeat business" that comes to a continuing education unit in terms of the continued enrollments in related programs and the requests to develop new programs by institutional and community leaders. In my own institution, we have built a reputation over the last seven years for high-quality programs in alcohol and drug studies, which we assess by using all of the measurement techniques described above. Our confidence is also based on the many employers who call upon us for in-house programs, our local newspaper's invitation to cosponsor a major, communitywide educational effort on treatment alternatives, and the number of contracts on which government agencies invite us to bid. Internally, as well as in the eyes of key faculty and community leaders, these are all indications that we provide high-quality programs. In general, what is most important is that a continuing education unit talk about evaluation, seek feedback, and have systematic ways to communicate its service to the knowledge needs of individuals, institutions, and the community.

Regularly Updating the Curriculum

A final necessity for quality assurance is a method for updating the curriculum and instruction as knowledge changes or as the potential applications of the knowledge change. Student and employer evaluations help here, but the most effective means is regular interaction with advisory committees. On a yearly basis, it is important to report to advisory committees in order to provide them with program progress and enrollment information as well as to solicit their input on content and instruction issues. The programmer must rely on advisers' reactions not only to data provided by the continuing education unit but also to what they "hear" in the field. These contacts with advisers can be valuable exchanges for curricular updates and for explorations of new program ideas that advisers bring from their respective professional contexts. The contact establishes continuity and collegiality between the programmer and his or her advisory groups. It also creates an opportunity for university faculty and practitioners to get together periodically, even to pursue separate agendas. These interactions can result in the identification of new research topics by faculty, gifts of equipment or cash to a department, enhanced knowledge about employment opportunities for graduates, and even shared projects.

When a certificate program appears to have run its course, based on declining student demand and diminishing leadership interest, the programmer must gracefully find a way to terminate it and to move on to new projects. One of the great advantages of continuing higher education is that we can respond so effectively to educational needs and cease an investment of time and resources when a need has been fully met.

Conclusion: Guiding Principles

There is no formula for quality, and given the diversity of higher education institutions in the United States, it would be presumptuous to articulate any fixed guidelines. Nonetheless, this chapter has suggested some general parameters for assessing quality certificate programs: (1) taking the time to build an intellectually solid advisory group for designing the curriculum, identifying faculty, and thinking through methodology; (2) involving, as appropriate, practitioners, stakeholders, and beneficiaries of the program in its design, implementation, and evaluation; and (3) being creative in evaluating the effectiveness of the program and regularly reviewing and updating the curriculum.

These are simple principles, perhaps, but they are often forgotten in the rush to get to market with the hottest new idea. Time invested in thinking, planning, shaping ideas, recruiting good instructors, and building diverse teaching resources will greatly enhance quality. With quality also comes program longevity, reputation, and profitability.

Reference

Robinson, J. H. *The Whats, Hows, and Benefits of Noncredit Certificate Programs.* Manhattan, Kans.: Learning Resources Network, 1991.

Mary Lindenstein Walshok is associate vice chancellor for extended studies and public service and adjunct associate professor, Department of Sociology, University of California, San Diego.

Favorable cost-benefit ratios of certificate programs in part explain the popularity and growth of this new enterprise among colleges, universities, and professional groups.

The Economics of Certificate Programs

Jane Hoopes Robinson

Economic benefits are as important as the satisfaction of student needs to the success of certificate programs. Economic power in fact drives the creation and maintenance of these programs, regardless of whether they are credit or noncredit. To continue serving student needs, certificate programs must bring appropriate economic benefits to the sponsoring organizations.

As described in other chapters of this volume, credit and noncredit certificate programs have allowed sponsoring educational and professional organizations to design curricula that differ from those of the traditional degree programs. In general, these sponsoring organizations have developed shorter, better targeted, and more flexible curricula, "guided" to meet the needs of specific groups. The result has been certificate programs that mutually benefit students, their employers, and the sponsoring organizations—colleges, universities, and other institutions such as the American Banking Association and the Credit Union National Association.

Although certificate programs have undergone extraordinary growth during the past decade, it is very difficult to acquire accurate data about the programs on a national basis. Thus, the task of writing about the economics of certificate programs requires the use of limited data and observations to assess economic value.

Credit Certificate Programs

Available in a wide array of topics, credit certificate programs vary from original program designs to existing courses put together to form a certificate.

Economic Benefits to Sponsoring Organizations. Undergraduate and graduate certificate programs have economic value for traditional educational institutions. For example, in creating the kinds of certificate programs that students want, institutions have increased enrollments by drawing students to specific areas of study and by sometimes converting students mildly interested in a subject into serious majors. In other cases, the opportunity to earn a certificate has attracted new students who want a short program of study or an extra credential, such as the dental assistant or the postgraduate accounting certificate. Another benefit in terms of enrollment rates has been the recruitment of students who originally plan to come for a one- or two-year certificate and then decide to continue working for a traditional degree.

Flexibility in shaping and offering certificate programs has been another source of economic benefit. By creating postgraduate certificate programs that draw on existing courses within major program areas (such as accounting or public management), public institutions have not had to seek approval from state commissions on higher education, as required for permanent degree programs. Because the formal approval route is costly in time and effort, certificate programs have helped institutions move into and out of the marketplace as demand dictates. For example, Indiana University did not award the postgraduate accounting certificate in 1984–1985 but awarded it to twenty-three people in 1989–1990; the university has not awarded a certificate in secretarial studies since 1985–1986, when it was awarded to one individual.

In some cases, certificate programs have allowed institutions to experiment with new program areas before making a greater, long-term commitment. A good example is environmental studies.

Since 1984, Indiana University has awarded about 2,500 credit certificates. For the Indiana University system (eight campuses), the increase was 26 percent (from 376 in 1984–1985 to 474 in 1989–1990). In the past three years, certificates have constituted 3 percent of the degrees/credentials awarded by the university. Based on data available and the increasingly competitive global economy, this growth should continue.

Throughout Indiana, public educational institutions have awarded about 22,000 certificates during the past ten years. Most of these have been awarded by two-year institutions, especially by the vocational and technical colleges. Between 1979 and 1989, the number of certificates awarded increased 11 percent (1,788 to 1,988), although the three peak years were from 1982 to 1985. The increase and decrease in this bulge were due mainly to the number of certificates awarded for allied health. Fields such as engineering technologies and mechanics also followed this general pattern. Business and office management certificates did the same but still ended up much higher in percentage increase (from 486 to 712, or 46 percent) over this time period.

The National Center for Education Statistics (Carpenter, 1989) reported that institutions of higher education nationwide had awarded nearly 11,000 certificates in 1986–1987. Of these, 6,700 were postbaccalaureate and 4,267 were post-master's certificates. Fee income plus state allocations for credit hours represented considerable income.

Economic Benefits to Recipients. Just as individuals with college degrees have greater earning power than do individuals without degrees, those with certificates can have greater earning power depending on the field of study. For example, because accountants are in demand, a post-graduate certificate in accounting makes a student with a general business administration degree more attractive to potential employers. At a minimum, certificates give recipients credentials that they might otherwise not have and officially indicate to employers areas of specialized study that may increase the recipients' ability to find suitable positions.

Budgeting. Because many certificate programs require less time to complete than the two- or four-year degree programs, their indirect administrative costs (costs to recruit, counsel, enroll, and keep records for a student) are somewhat higher than those for degree programs. This statement assumes that it costs as much to recruit and matriculate a student who will be enrolled for one year as it does for one who will stay for four years. At Indiana University, for example, fees for courses in certificates are the same as those for any other credit courses, with income determined by the fee set per credit hour. In some cases, special laboratory fees are assessed. Because many credit certificate programs have been created by combining existing courses into different configurations—East Asian Studies, International Studies, and Public Management, for example—the required courses are already available. Thus, a certificate program has added no fixed operating costs such as new buildings or tenured faculty lines.

In order to determine whether a certificate will add fixed operating costs and break even, one must examine the following areas: (1) *income:* How many students are enrolled? How many credit hours? At what rate per hour? Will rate per hour vary with program or special equipment? Does a special equipment or materials fee need to be assessed, and if so, how much? (2) *planning and designing the certificate:* How much faculty time will be required? How much faculty ego and ownership are involved and at what cost? (The ego costs can have indirect time and political costs when top administrators have to coach and counsel faculty to get them to either let go of a program idea or allow the idea to be changed.) Will various campus committees expend effort in discussion and review? Will the development cost of the program be assessed in the first year only or divided over several years? (3) *faculty:* Will new faculty be needed or can the new students be absorbed into existing courses? If new faculty are needed, will the new program require new faculty lines (fixed expense) or funds for adjuncts (variable expense)? (4) *special accreditation:* Does the certificate require this accreditation? If so, from whom, how often, and at what cost?

(5) *equipment:* Will existing equipment and facilities be suitable? If not, what are the costs of new space and equipment? (6) *student services* (counseling, registration, and recordkeeping): Can the new students be handled by current staff or will the increased enrollment require new full- or part-time staff? (7) *promotion:* Can the certificate program be absorbed into the standard catalogue at little or no added cost? Does it require special promotional brochures and advertising (variable cost)?

Exhibit 4.1, a sample budget for a graduate certificate, illustrates both a method of budget construction and the financial advantage of creating a certificate around existing courses. The forty-six students used in this model are presumed to be students who would not have entered a two-year master's program; thus, attracting any or all of these students into existing courses is a straightforward net gain.

Exhibit 4.1. Sample Budget for a Graduate Public Management Certificate

Year 1 Income

46 students at 9 hours each for each of two semesters	414	
	2	
Credit hours	828	
Cost per hour	60	
		$49,680
Technology/computer fee per student	25	
	46	
		$1,150
		$50,830

Expenses

Planning and designing	
Faculty costs are fixed; thus, either no cost or that of released time and payment to adjust for possibly one course	$1,600
Faculty existing and courses existing	0
New equipment	0
Student services fixed	
Promotion shared with other programs	$200
	$1,800
Net or contribution margin to fixed costs	$49,030

In summary, to the extent that credit certificate programs provide economic benefits to the institutions, the students, and the communities that they serve, they will continue to grow in number and enrollments. Clearly, they allow educational organizations other options for serving new, existing, and postdegree students.

Noncredit Certificate Programs

Noncredit certificate programs are usually found in the continuing education (CE) programs of colleges, universities, and professional organizations. In both public and private institutions, CE units are often self-supporting— that is, they receive no state funds for any building or personnel costs. Thus, they have a strong economic motive to promote noncredit certificates, which sometimes makes these certificates more visible than those in many credit programs. This can also occur because the credit programs tend to promote two- and four-year degree programs more heavily than certificates.

For CE units that have designed and offered noncredit certificates, the economic impetus is clear, that is, the opportunity to gain income subsidized by state funds or other parts of a dues-paying organization. In the mid 1970s, only a few organizations such as the New York University School of Continuing Studies offered noncredit certificates. Now, hundreds of CE programs and some professional organizations offer noncredit certificates. Increased enrollments indicate that student and employer needs are creating a desire for the certificates, and institutions are responding to those needs and to the opportunity to attract new income.

With world economic conditions in flux and openings for white-collar jobs becoming more competitive, students view certificate programs as a way to acquire new skills and knowledge through well-designed curricula and to document the study with credentials. Joining user needs with the capability and flexibility of noncredit CE courses, programmers have able to design the curricula in a timely manner that has ensured expansion of the market for new and existing noncredit certificates.

Although the National Center for Education Statistics collects data on certificates awarded for credit study, no data are available on noncredit certificates. Thus, examination of CE catalogues and other written materials and interviews with CE personnel are the only ways to assess the growth and economic value of noncredit certificate programs.

Economic Benefits to Sponsoring Organizations. As with credit certificate programs, noncredit certificate programs also have strong income potential for sponsoring organizations: colleges, universities, private corporations, and professional organizations. In the eyes of many, the potential for these organizations to develop and offer certificates has just barely been tapped. Also, since many noncredit programs in higher education and professional organizations are not directly subsidized, the economic impetus to offer noncredit certificates is being discovered by increasingly greater numbers of organizations.

For many years, New York University, which now offers more than seventy noncredit certificate programs, has served as a model for many smaller institutions in the development of their own certificate programs. With each passing year, as program catalogues show a greater number and diversity of noncredit certificates, it is increasingly apparent that these programs generate income for the sponsors, especially as the legitimacy of their entire noncredit programs is established and thus enrollments in seminars and courses increase.

Unlike many credit certificate programs, noncredit certificate programs typically do not have prerequisites; thus, students determine their readiness and can attend any course or seminar within a certificate program. In addition, a guided or well-planned curriculum in a particular certificate program can attract new students who may then decide to complete the multipart program, thus again increasing the income of the sponsor. Moreover, because some colleges and universities award credit for selected noncredit certificates—either their own or those of programs approved by the American Council on Education—they have also benefited by attracting new students into their degree programs.

Along with colleges and universities, professional organizations are well positioned to take advantage of the increasing interest in noncredit certificate programs. First, many of these organizations design materials to prepare people for professional certification examinations. Although they need to avoid confusing the value of their national certification with the value of certificate programs, they can gain economic benefits by selling these materials to colleges and universities to use as the basis for noncredit certificates. For example, the quality management and the production and inventory management certificate programs offered by Indiana University at South Bend utilize materials from the local chapters of the American Society for Quality Control and the American Production and Inventory Control Society. Although the role of each stakeholder in these programs differs, each receives economic benefits: Students gain access to courses of study that may not be available in existing degree programs. Employers have access to a needed, live course of study for those unable or unwilling to enroll in a degree program. The CE unit attracts new students who need the knowledge and the certificates, and the unit may gain special credibility for its program. And the professional organizations gain through the higher visibility and credibility that derive from cooperation with a college or university, an increased potential for acquiring new members and more people aware of the testing and certificate programs available, an additional means for certified members to gain recertification points, a new market for their books and materials, and awards to local chapters for expanded educational activities.

Second, professional organizations have also recognized the income potential of noncredit certificates. For example, both the American Institute of Banking (AIB) and the Credit Union National Association (CUNA) have developed certificate programs for their members. AIB offers both diploma and certificate programs. Diplomas are awarded for professional development programs that relate to specific banking departments such as commercial and mortgage lending; certificates are awarded for completing a curriculum in general skill areas such as customer service and supervision.

Although the structures of the two certificate programs differ—AIB has designed extensive multicourse programs while CUNA offers certificates for attending several-day schools—each organization markets multitopic certificate programs that must pay their own way. Both have significant longevity (AIB offered its first certificate program over eighty years ago and CUNA almost forty years ago) and have seen healthy growth. AIB's growth occurred mainly in the 1970s and CUNA's in the past decade. For example, CUNA has doubled the number of sections in its programs from sixteen to thirty-two since 1985. With enrollments varying from 50 to 150 per program, the economics of offering certificate programs has been proven. AIB has over 155,000 involved in its diploma/certificate programs. Both AIB and CUNA programs are designed to serve their member organizations exclusively and are open only to their employees or specially approved people such as private-practice attorneys employed by the member organizations.

Economic Benefits to Recipients. A primary motivation for people to earn noncredit certificates is the expectation of economic gain, whether incurred directly from receipt of the certificate or from application of the noncredit certificate toward a two- or four-year degree (occasionally for no additional cost). For example, a secretary at a Fortune 500 company in north central Indiana became a professional contract administrator after receiving her paralegal studies certificate. Another legal secretary at a Fortune 500 company was promoted to a paralegal position. Another person was promoted to production manager after completing the production and inventory management certificate.

For some students, noncredit certificates from either a professional organization or a college or university have enabled them to be promoted without having traditional degrees. Because most noncredit certificate programs do not require nearly as much time or money as do degree programs, a student benefits economically both from the career move and the reduced amount of time and fees.

Since some student and employer benefits occur indirectly, they are harder to measure. For example, a noncredit certificate in paralegal studies gave one Indiana University recipient greater professional legitimacy, greater exposure to people higher up in the organization, and more authority to make decisions; it also established new criteria in the job description and, in general, increased the employee's value to the employer for greater job security.

External financial support can be another indirect benefit. If a student is employed and the certificate area is job related, many employers will pay all fees. In circumstances where credit courses are not specifically work related and thus employers will not pay tuition, depending on the placement record, the concentration of time, and whether the noncredit courses can be applied toward a degree, the student may be eligible for several kinds of financial assistance such as Veterans Administration or student loans.

Because administrators of noncredit certificates often have greater program design flexibility than is available to administrators of credit certificates, structure and content of noncredit certificates can be revised more quickly and often with fewer layers of bureaucratic approval. Thus, students and employers involved in such certificate programs can not only request but more easily get a curriculum designed to fit the needs of their specific competitive marketplace.

Budgeting. Most noncredit programs operate on a self-supporting basis, paying all direct and indirect costs. Unlike the traditional credit-fee structure, pricing for each noncredit program can vary per contact hour for courses and seminars and can vary according to potential audience size and ability to pay. The laws of supply and demand, coupled with the image or prestige of the organization, determine pricing. Income will be generated if the certificate program topic and structure meet a real need, the sponsoring unit has credibility, the price is acceptable, and the timing and promotion are right.

As in budgeting for credit certificates, the organization must determine whether a noncredit certificate program will add to fixed operating costs and break even. This requires an examination of the following areas: (1) *income:* How many students are enrolled? How many contact hours? At what rate per hour? Will rate per hour vary with program or special equipment? Does a special equipment or materials fee need to be assessed, and if so, how much? (2) *planning and designing the certificate:* Can this task be performed by existing staff or will external consultants be required? (3) *faculty:* Full time (fixed expense) or adjunct (variable expense)? (4) *accreditation:* Is accreditation needed, and if so, how often and how much? (5) *institutional overhead:* Is it assessed on a per student or annual gross basis and can student fees absorb this cost? (6) *student services* (counseling, registration, recordkeeping, and mailing): Can the students be handled by current staff (fixed expense) or will the task require new full-time (fixed expense) or part-time (variable expense) staff? (7) *promotion:* Can the standard catalogue absorb the promotion as part of a fixed cost or is special promotion (separate brochures, letters, and advertising) required? (8) *payment to cooperating professional organization:* Is this payment required, and if so, on what basis and how much? (9) *possible staff or faculty travel:* Does the accreditation require attending a meeting of the organization? Does staying current require attending trade shows or professional meetings?

A sample budget for a noncredit certificate is shown in Exhibit 4.2. As with many noncredit certificates, the organization is attracting new students and has minimal direct program development costs; that is, development costs are absorbed through existing fixed (administrative staff) costs.

Exhibit 4.2. Sample Budget for a Noncredit Quality Management Certificate

Year 1 Income

51 students at $25 (one-time registration fee)		$1,275
26 students[a] for each of	26	
2 courses for each of	2	
	52	
2 semesters	2	
	104	
(estimated 25/hours/course × $10/hour)	25	$2,600
	10	
		$26,000
20 students in 2 one-day seminars $195		
(40 × $195)		$7,800
		$35,075

Expenses

Indirect only, since development of new program is part of professional staff responsibility	0
Record keeping same as program development	0
Special brochure for each of 2 seminars at $1000 each	$2,000
General catalogue: 100 per course (4), seminar (2), and certificate (2) (4 courses and 2 seminars at $100 each plus certificate description twice)	$800
Faculty cost $30/hour × estimate 25 hours for each of 4 courses	$3,000
Faculty seminar 2 at $500/day	$1,000
	$6,800
Net or contribution margin to fixed/indirect costs	$28,275

[a]Not all students take courses each semester.

Overall Economic Value. Where appropriately designed, conducted with quality, integrity, and credibility, and tailored to the marketplace, noncredit certificate programs have economic benefits for all parties: sponsoring organizations, individuals, and employers. And given the increasingly competitive push for continuous improvement to satisfy the customer, the demand for credentials—including certificates—will continue to grow. For employees to "stay the same" will mean that they will not "stay around."

Reference

Carpenter, J. *Completions in Institutions of Higher Education, 1986–87.* National Center for Education Statistics Report no. 90–322. Washington, D.C.: U.S. Department of Education, Office of Educational Research and Improvement, 1989.

Jane Hoopes Robinson is director of the Division of Continuing Education, Indiana University, South Bend. She is also author of Certificate Programs, *published by LERN.*

*As a new millennium approaches, new types of certificate programs
in continuing higher education will be developed. Among the
current policies and procedures affecting the development and
implementation of certificate programs at traditional colleges and
universities, some will support and others will hinder this growth.*

Institutional Policies and Procedures: Bridges or Barriers?

John C. Snider, Francine Marasco, Donna Keene

As we move toward the twenty-first century, administrators and staff of
continuing higher education programs need to understand thoroughly the
constituencies who will be served, the programs that will be offered, and
the delivery techniques that will be utilized. The accelerating rate of change
in the twenty-first century and the explosive development of new technology will foster unprecedented growth in noncredit education. In particular,
new types of certificate programs will be the order of the day (Snider,
1990). The success of these new programs, whether they are designed in
the public or private sector, higher education, or the corporate world, will
depend on the educational environments in which they are engineered.
When policies, attitudes, and resources foster and reward innovative ideas
and creative programs, success will be readily achieved. In contrast, when
policies and procedures restrain and limit, success will be achieved only
by hurdling numerous barriers. It thus follows that institutions of higher
education that embrace the philosophy of innovation and creativity will be
able to develop the kinds of policies and procedures needed to bridge the
gap between conceptualization and implementation.

The purpose of this chapter is to examine current policies and procedures to determine what they might reveal about the design of future certificate programs. Since there is a dearth of information on these programs
in academia, as noted by our coeditors Holt and Lopos, we included in our

We are grateful to Craig Pearson, our study statistician, the National University
Continuing Education Association, and Peterson's Guides, Inc., for their assistance.

literature search publications from the American Society of Association Executives (ASAE). ASAE is an organization with twenty thousand individual members, who represent approximately eight thousand associations. One of ASAE's main purposes is to serve as a resource to its members, advising them on how to organize and manage their respective associations. The ASAE also publishes a trade magazine, *Association Management*, featuring timely, relevant articles. ASAE proved a useful resource in researching leads on certificate programs. When referring to ASAE materials in this chapter, the terms *certification* and *certificate program* are used interchangeably.

History of Certification Programs

Professional certification programs have existed since the Middle Ages, when the thirteenth-century Holy Roman emperor Frederick II developed a credentialing program for physicians. In the United States, the earliest certification programs appeared in the field of education. They were affiliated with churches to ensure that schoolmasters held orthodox religious beliefs. As the nation grew, communities established their own criteria for teachers, which varied considerably. Shortly after World War II, the National Education Association of the United States began a movement to develop uniform professional standards for teachers. A wide variety of types and levels of teacher certification still exist today. In the past thirty years, federal and state governments have worked to ensure high standards of teacher preparation, to improve the certification process, and to establish uniform requirements. The development of teacher certification helped establish the present multidisciplinary certification movement. Unlike teacher certification, however, certification in many professions is not a government-regulated licensing mechanism (Gilley, 1985).

As gleaned from information disseminated by ASAE (1988), we submit for consideration here three summaries of reasons that professional organizations establish certification programs: (1) The *objectives of a certification program* are to raise the standards of a profession, encourage self-assessment by offering guidelines for achievement, identify persons with acceptable knowledge of principles and practices of the profession and related disciplines, award recognition to those who have demonstrated a high level of competence and ethical fitness for a profession, and improve the performance in the profession by encouraging participation in a continuing program of professional development. (2) The *benefits of certification to the individual* are increased self-esteem, increased respect and recognition in the industry or profession, increased opportunity for upward mobility and enhancement of ability to compete in the job market, increased remuneration and job benefits, and increased professional credibility. (3) The *benefits of certification to an association* are that it reinforces membership loyalty to the association, indicates the association's sincerity in promoting professionalism, serves as a source of income, encourages the orderly and efficient collection and consolidation of the body of knowledge, increases member interest in continuing education, and provides a vehicle to reward members who develop a high level of professionalism.

Since the late 1960s, many states have passed legislation requiring licensed professionals to participate in continuing professional education on a periodic basis in order to be relicensed. Some observers believed that this mandatory continuing education (MCE) was to be only an interim solution, and opponents of the MCE movement have argued that it does not necessarily improve competence. Yet, after two decades, the number of states passing MCE legislation has continued to grow. Given the many factors that influence the performance and competence of professionals, it is hard to generalize about the effects of continuing professional education on competence. Nevertheless, evidence gathered from research studies, anecdotes, and related information from a variety of professions shows that (1) continuing education can affect performance, (2) the greatest effect of MCE is on those who do not place importance on updating their careers, since it obliges them to fulfill certain requirements, (3) MCE has brought about a proliferation of programs, and (4) more attention is being focused on competence (Phillips, 1987).

The following sixteen professions are ranked by the number of states requiring MCE in that field: certified public accountants, 47; optometrists, 46; nursing home administrators, 43; pharmacists, 38; real estate brokers, 32; lawyers, 28; veterinarians, 26; physicians, 21; social workers, 20; psychologists, 15; dentists, 13; nurses, 11; licensed practical nurses, 11; physical therapists, 7; engineers (professional), 1; and architects, 1 (Phillips, 1987, p. 74). To set the stage for our study, and to conclude our review of the literature, it should be noted that ASAE (1987) surveyed its membership and found that 290 of their member associations offer some form of certificate program.

A Study of Program Policies and Practices: Goals, Methods, and Limitations

With the above information in mind, it is reasonable to assert that continuing education practitioners based at traditional universities and colleges must continue to collaborate in assisting people with their professional certification needs. We believe that by describing certain characteristics of certificate programs relating to policies and practices, we can help continuing education practitioners plan for the future. Therefore, the major goal of our study was to examine current policies and practices in order to determine what purposes they might serve in the design and development of certificate programs. More specifically, our aim was threefold: (1) to gain an overall view of current policies and practices, (2) to provide a data base for later comparisons, and (3) to provide input to policies and practices.

To collect the necessary data, a survey instrument was designed, with traditional colleges and universities as the targeted audience. We invited all of the member institutions of the National University Continuing Education Association (NUCEA) to participate in this study. One of the principal reasons that we selected this pool of institutions for our study was that the quality of the institutions was assured by virtue of their accreditation and affiliation with NUCEA. Members of NUCEA are primarily degree-granting institutions of higher education accredited either by one of the six regional accrediting associations that hold membership in the Council on Postsecondary Accreditation (COPA) or, with the approval of the board of directors, by another accrediting agency that holds membership in COPA. In addition, all member institutions have substantial programs in continuing education.

NUCEA provided labels of the member colleges and universities devoted to continuing higher education and public service. All of the programs and courses of these institutions are covered by their respective accreditations. Inasmuch as Lopos and Holt (1988) previously surveyed this same population, our study can be viewed as a follow-up to their earlier survey.

A total of 388 institutions received a cover letter of invitation, copies of the two-part survey instrument, and a self-addressed, postage-paid return envelope. The first part of the survey instrument was designed to be completed by the NUCEA institutional representative, since the data requested were general demographics. The second part of the survey instrument was designed to be completed by those people directly responsible for certificate programs. Of the total 388 NUCEA institutional representatives, 131 survey forms were returned, thus slightly more than 33 percent of the total population was included in the study.

Although 131 forms were returned, some of them did not include both parts of the survey instrument, and others did not include responses to every item. Therefore, one limitation of the study was that the totals reported did not always equal 100 percent. Another limitation was that the manner in which some of the items were answered was not always in accord with the manner in which we intended the items to be interpreted. Therefore, the results and conclusions of this study may be limited in applicability to this particular sample population.

Once the data were collected, they were entered into personal computer files, and, through use of commercial software packages, the following data reports were generated and statistical tests applied: (1) Frequency reports in the form of pie charts were generated for variables incorporating percentages. (2) Means were calculated for selected variables. (3) A correlation matrix was generated to test the relationship of selected variables.

Core Demographic Survey. For Part One of the survey instrument,

"Core Demographic Data Survey Instrument," of the 131 survey forms returned, only 109 included core demographic data.

Public or Private. We found that 81.7 percent of the sample represented public institutions, while 18.3 percent represented private institutions. Moreover, 13.9 percent of the institutions serviced the local area, 40.7 percent serviced a regional area, 32.4 percent serviced statewide areas, and 13 percent considered themselves nationwide providers of service.

Surrounding Area. Regarding the populations of the areas surrounding the institutions, we found that 37.6 percent were in an area of up to 100,000; 14.7 percent were located in an area of 100,001–250,000; 10.1 percent were in an area of 250,001–500,000; 13.8 percent were in an area of 500,001–1 million; 10.1 percent were in an area of 1–2 million; and 15 percent were in an area of over 2 million. In other words, 62.4 percent of the institutions were located in areas of 500,000 or less people.

Enrollment. Size of enrollments of the institutions was the next item of interest. Enrollment size of the population was less than 1,000 for 4.6 percent of the institutions; 1,001–2,500 for 7.3 percent; 2,501–5,000 for 12.8 percent; 5,001–10,000 for 22.2 percent; 10,001–15,000 for 19.3 percent; 15,001–20,000 for 12.8 percent; 20,001–25,000 for .08 percent; and 25,000 or more for 12.8 percent. In other words, nearly 47 percent of the participating institutions had enrollments under 10,000 students, while the rest enrolled over 10,000.

Administrative Location. We also sought information describing where the continuing education unit was administratively located at each institution. The majority of units, 83 percent, were located within campuswide continuing education divisions. Another 1 percent were housed at colleges of business, and the other 15 percent were located in other academic divisions, schools, or colleges.

Programming. A breakdown of program types in current programming areas, as well as in future plans for the next medium-range planning period (three- to five-year span), was the next area of interest. While many individuals in continuing education have predicted growth, apparently without the benefit of hard data, those who responded in our sample clearly indicated continued expansion of noncredit certificate programs. Specifically, sample institutions relied on noncredit certificate programming, on the average, 9.3 percent of the time, and reliance on this activity within three to five years was expected to increase to 13 percent. At the same time, the percentage of conferences and institutes that award certificates was expected to increase by almost 1 percent. Another significant growth area of which continuing education practitioners should be aware is special executive development certificates. Those who responded to the survey question regarding the breakdown of program types and the participants involved in current programming areas relied on this area of programming, on the average, for 16 percent of their total programming. However, respondents indicated that programming for special executive development was expected to increase to 20 percent during the next 3 to 5 years. Overall, top administrators predicted increased growth in noncredit certificate programs by approximately 7 percent during the next 3 to 5 years.

Teaching Methods. When we asked the institutions about their teaching techniques, we found that most of them relied on traditional classroom techniques 76 percent of the time, but that, on the average, they utilized a form of nontraditional instruction such as case studies or internships 10 percent of the time. Furthermore, those same institutions relied on computer-based training, on the average, 4.5 percent of the time, while videotape instruction was used only 3 percent of the time, and teleconferencing was used only 2.8 percent of the time. The rest of the time, the institutions used other techniques for imparting instruction, for example, distance learning through correspondence.

Course Evaluations. By querying "What program evaluation/follow-up techniques do you use for the majority of your programs?" we were able to determine that 95 percent of the 107 respondents utilized a course satisfaction survey and that 45.8 percent conducted cost-benefit analyses, while approximately 24 percent evaluated performance change and utilized long-term evaluations. Another 11.2 percent measured skills transfer. Of the 34 programs that measured skills transfer, 26 were noncredit. Since certificate programs typically evaluate the individual, the measurements of skills transfer are most likely consistent across programs.

Target Audience. To gather data on the target audiences for the certificate programs, we asked the participants to provide percentages regarding certain audiences. About 17.6 percent of the population reported that small businesses were the leading target audience of all of the programs. The other main audiences were government, 12.2 percent; education, 11.7 percent; health care, 9.5 percent; and services, 9.5 percent.

Finance. Fiscal policies were then tabulated among the institutions that responded. We found that 45.2 percent of the institutions were self-supporting units, while 36.5 percent were expected to generate a surplus to underwrite other activities. Only 15.4 percent were established to provide a service and operate within a given budget. Our data indicate that the self-supporting units averaged slightly more programs than did those that were created to provide a service and operate within a given budget. However, the mere number of programs may not indicate productivity or complexity. This area requires further study.

In order to learn more about the economics of the survey participants, we included an item on revenues generated during the last reporting year. A total of 102 institutions responded, and we were able to determine that over 59 percent of our participants generated between $500,000 and $6 million. At the opposite ends of the spectrum, we learned that .05 percent generated less than $100,000, and a small percentage, .02 percent, generated from $30 million to $50 million.

Big Business. As the above figures indicate, continuing education is big business (see Robinson, this volume). Phillips (1987, p. 74) has noted, moreover, that "continuing education is the hot area in today's education community. Recent studies show that spending on continuing or adult education will soon become the largest percentage of total education spending for the first time in U.S. history."

In addition to revenues generated during the last reporting year, we also asked about the program sources of the revenues. The results showed that nearly 31 percent were derived from credit programs awarding grades only, while 17 percent were generated from credit programs awarding certificates as well as grades. Thus, 47.9 percent of the institutions derived their revenues from credit programs. From noncredit courses awarding certificates, institutions derived 12.4 percent of their revenues, and from noncredit courses awarding no certificates, 20.6 percent. Thus, 33 percent of total revenues were derived from noncredit programs. Almost 11 percent of the revenues were derived from conferences and institutes. These figures appear to also reflect the breakdown of program activity.

Current and Future Status of Certificate Programs. As previously stated, Part Two of the survey instrument was designed to be completed by the administrators directly responsible for the certificate programs. We believed that the certificate administrators would be more familiar with program details and thus respond more accurately to the program details than would the chief administrators.

Credit or Noncredit. A total of 302 institutions returned Part Two, and 39 percent reported that the certificate programs described were noncredit, while approximately 56 percent were credit programs and 5 percent were both credit and noncredit certificate programs.

Program Areas. At the beginning of the survey instrument, respondents were asked to supply the titles of their programs. When the data were collected, the titles were grouped and categorized. The following are the program categories and their rank order by percentages: business and management, 31 percent; business administrative support, 10 percent; engineering or engineering related, 9 percent; public affairs, 8 percent; computer or information science, 7 percent; allied health and health science, 6 percent; and education, 5 percent.

Degree or Nondegree. Almost 64 percent of the respondents reported that their certificate programs were not allowed to form part of a degree program, while 36 percent of the certificate programs were allowed to form part of a credit degree program.

Certificate. In addition, we wanted to learn who signed the certificate and if there was more than one signature on it. The respondents reported that 54 percent of the time the dean signed the certificate, while the program administrator responsible for the certificate program signed 20 percent of the time, and the president or the provost signed 16 percent of the time. When a second signature was placed on the certificate, the program administrator's signature was the most likely to appear, at 40 percent of the time. The dean's signature was the second most likely, at 23 percent of the time. The president or the provost provided the second signature 12 percent of the time, a noninstitutional representative provided the second signature 11 percent of the time, and, last, an assistant dean or department head signed the certificate 6 percent of the time. It is noteworthy that noninstitutional representatives signed certificates, since this fact indicates a definite trend of collaboration with outside organizations.

Cooperative Programs. The involvement of traditional universities and colleges with outside agencies was further reaffirmed when we found that 50 percent of our respondents identified external agencies or associations as cosponsors or supporters of specific certificate programs. That these institutions were able to nurture ongoing relationships with external organizations indicates flexibility in their policies and procedures. Some of the categories of outside agencies, and their respective percentages of identification within our sample, are as follows: management associations, 17 percent; general government, 15 percent; education, 13 percent; hospitals or health care, 9 percent; and law, 9 percent.

Program Formats. In answer to our questions about scheduling formats, we found that daytime classes were slightly ahead of evening classes (59 percent to 56 percent), and weekend courses (33 percent) came in last. A small percentage (10 percent) of respondents utilized correspondences courses, and an even smaller percentage (6 percent) used telecommunications. We also learned that 75 percent of the certificate programs were offered year-round with continuous enrollment, and 25 percent were offered only at certain set intervals.

For completion of certificate programs, institutional requirements varied. If a program was government related, then the institution set standards according to governmental regulations. If a certificate program was for credit, a number of credit hours were required. Often, an internship, practicum, or laboratory work was included as a requirement for the certificate. If the certificate was issued in a joint effort with an agency or association, then it had to be approved by the external agency as well as by the institution. The passing of tests or exams appeared to be the most common requirement on campuses. In a few instances, residencies were listed as requirements, and often times, attendance was the only requirement. The strictest requirement reported was completion of a thesis.

Grading. Each certificate program administrator was asked about methods of evaluating program participants. The majority (72 percent) evaluated with tests, and another 35 percent evaluated with reports. Observation was used 32 percent of the time, whereas measurement of competencies such as in-class performance of knowledge, presentations, and so on, occurred 25 percent of the time.

Since testing was frequently used, it was also reported that in most certificate programs (66 percent) letters or numbers were used to grade the tests. Respondents also let us know that a pass-or-fail system of grading was used 25 percent of the time. A combination of letters and numbers and pass-or-fail grades was used 7 percent of the time. Upon the students' completion of the certificate programs, we fond that institutions recorded the completion 74 percent of the time, while the others provided a diploma or certificate without recording completion on a transcript. Requirements for student enrollment in certificate programs in 50 percent of the institutions were a high school diploma, a general education diploma, or experiential learning. For only 6 percent of the institutions, a bachelor's degree was required, and a professional license was required in yet a smaller percentage of institutions. Graduate degrees were not required for enrollment in any of the certificate programs.

Instructor Credentials. Requirements for instructors of the certificate programs formed another area of investigation. Among our survey participants, 36 percent required master's degrees, and 15 percent required only bachelor's degrees. Another 23 percent required prior teaching experience, and only 7 percent required a professional certificate.

Tuition. We also asked the administrators of the programs how their certificate programs were paid for by students, and we found that in 42 percent of the certificate programs no financial aid was available from the institution. Most of the certificate programs (45 percent) were employer sponsored. In approximately 30 percent of the programs, grants, guaranteed student loans, veterans' benefits, and scholarships assisted the certificate program participants.

Residency. We then asked whether on-campus residence was required to complete the programs. For 94 percent of the programs, on-campus residency was not required. Furthermore, there was housing available to students enrolled in certificate programs on 19 percent of the campuses.

Location. Geographical restraints on the locations of the certificate programs were of interest. Some institutions maintained policies restraining program administrators from offering program locations where sister institutions might be offering the same program. For 74 percent of the certificate programs represented in the sample, there were no geographical restraints, while for 26 percent of the sample, there were.

Study Results: Implications, Conclusions, and Future Studies

During the 1980s, conventional wisdom predicted the growth of certificate programs, and this study confirmed the current increase in certificate programs as well as expected increases. Participants in this study predicted more growth in the special executive development programs, in particular.

Teaching techniques and evaluation techniques were basically traditional. As traditional education delivery techniques evolve in response to an increasingly high-technology environment, so too should teaching and evaluation techniques in continuing education certificate programs. The fact that 50 percent of the certificate program administrators in our sample were involved in cooperative efforts with external agencies indicates two important points: (1) institutional policies and procedures are flexible enough to allow such joint ventures, and (2) joint efforts allow universities to tailor certificate programs in order to meet the needs of specific groups.

Additionally, we found that self-supporting units administered more programs than did the units that were allocated budgets and had service as their main goal. As noted earlier, continuing education is big business. Consequently, self-supporting units will become more prevalent as budget cutbacks and funding restraints become more severe. Increases in the number and diversity of certificate programs are also indicated.

Traditional college and university continuing education units have significant opportunities ahead to improve assistance to adult students and professionals and to respond expeditiously to the explosive development of new technology. One area of opportunity involves taking advantage of academic networks and sharing resources and expertise. This practice will enable us to develop nationally recognized, standardized certificate programs for a variety of client groups. Clients will certainly benefit by being able to begin a certificate program at one institution and complete it at another. Another advantage of collaboration is standardization of proficiencies and competencies, which are difficult to identify at this time since each institution designs its own program.

By working more closely with external agencies, continuing education practitioners can set the stage for a winning scenario. Curriculum design, types of courses to be included, assessments and evaluations, sharing of instructors, and use of telecommunication (uplinks and downlinks) for delivery are all ways to achieve additional advantages for continuing education. Program quality will be enhanced and enriched. Moreover, the real beneficiaries will be our constituencies.

From this study, we have seen the need to continue research on such topics as ethical issues in higher continuing education, creative financing of continuing higher education, incentive compensation programs for continuing educators, periodical recertification, and legal problems with certification procedures.

Ethical issues concerning the quality of programs and instructors in continuing education have recently been a topic for discussion in the national media. While our sample of NUCEA institutions comprises the most prestigious programs in the country, many differences in requirements for instructors and students were noted, along with differences in duration of programs. Our findings on relationships with outside agencies and cosponsorships indicate that, indeed, creative financing is taking place. Since many continuing education units are self-supporting, incentive compensation programs come to mind.

Once we certify, do we ever recertify? This topic was not covered in our survey instrument, nor was the related topic of legal liability. That is, if we certify that someone is competent and in the work force, and he or she is subsequently shown to be otherwise, are we legally liable to the organization that hired the person?

Finally, the definitions of program activity, contact hours, numbers of participants, complexity of program logistics, and requirements for program completion are crucial topics in need of further examination. Clearly, as our study found, program activity is viewed in almost as many different ways as the number of participating institutions. The multitude of answers received in response to the question regarding program length underscored the complexities involved in "pigeon-holing" program descriptions.

These are all issues for future research. At present, our results illustrate the traditional quality of most certificate programs and a general consensus that certificate programs constitute a traditional or legitimate approach to education. Yet, the increased cooperation with outside organizations indicates that we have the ability and need to take risks in a rapidly changing educational marketplace. One matter is certain, continuing education practitioners have many opportunities to challenge existing institutional barriers and to bridge the gap between the present and the future.

References

American Society of Association Executives (ASAE). *Policies and Procedures in Association Management.* List No. 131. Washington, D.C.: ASAE, 1987.

American Society of Association Executives (ASAE). *Information Background Kit: Self-Regulation: Accreditation, Certification, and Standardization.* Washington, D.C.: ASAE, 1988.

Gilley, J. W. "Seeking the Common Pattern." *Association Management,* 1985, 37, 125–127.

Lopos, G. J., Holt, M. E., Bohlander, R. E., and Wells, J. H. (eds.). *Peterson's Guide to Certificate Programs at American Colleges and Universities.* Princeton, N.J.: Peterson's Guides, 1988.

Phillips, L. E. "Certifiably Educated." *Association Management,* 1987, 39, 73–76.

Snider, J. C. "Developing the Capabilities Needed to Address Future Challenges in Continuing Education." In D. Johnson (ed.), *Handbook on Professional Development.* Washington, D.C.: National University Continuing Education Association and Kellogg Foundation, 1990.

John C. Snider is dean in the College of Continuing Studies, University of Alabama, Tuscaloosa, and active in the National University Continuing Education Association.

Francine Marasco is program director in the Division of Professional and Management Development, College of Continuing Studies, University of Alabama.

Donna Keene is marketing account executive in the Division of Professional and Management Development, College of Continuing Studies, University of Alabama.

*Semistructured interviews with certificate program students
emphasized more positive than negative assessments, especially with
respect to the career-related values of such studies. Nonetheless,
the marginality of and limited receptivity to many certificate
programs within larger university structures raise concerns.*

Selected Interviews with Certificate Program Students

Thomas M. Rutkowski, Margaret E. Holt, George J. Lopos

The chapters in this volume clearly point to the growing need for, and popularity of, certificate programs in the United States. Nonetheless, these characterizations largely represent the perspectives of institutional representatives. Certainly, it is also important to ask how people who have completed certificate programs in recent years regard these educational experiences. A worthy and candid discussion of certificate programs should include firsthand information on the programs, gathered from actual participants. Thus, we decided to interview a number of individuals who had recently completed certificate programs.

Interviewing Certificate Recipients

Our work consisted of choosing a type of study, designing and testing a pilot instrument, making revisions of this instrument, selecting and interviewing the sample of certificate graduates, and analyzing the data gathered. We felt that it was essential for us to gather information about the programs in the respondents' own words, that their feelings and comments about their endeavors should not be confined by the bounds of a strict yes-no set of survey questions and answers. Thus, we chose a qualitative interview method for this study. Qualitative, open-ended questionnaires have been shown to yield data that are "descriptive," "rich," and "anecdotal" (Bogdan and Biklen, 1982), and this approach appeared to suit our needs.

Once we had settled on a general method, we prepared a pilot survey instrument. We then asked ten questions of a small sample (three) of successful participants in a representative certificate program sponsored

NEW DIRECTIONS FOR ADULT AND CONTINUING EDUCATION, no. 52, Winter 1991 © Jossey-Bass Inc., Publishers

by a large research university in the southeastern United States. The respondents, chosen from a list provided by the program's director, were interviewed by telephone without having prior knowledge of the questions. Two of the members of the sample for the pilot study had completed the courses in classes held at the university. The third person who was interviewed had taken the entire sequence of courses in a "correspondence" fashion, through the use of videotapes.

After the data from the pilot study were collected and analyzed, we revised some of the questions in an effort to elicit more discussion about the possibly unique features of certificate programs and about the quality of the programs. The questions eventually used in the actual study were structured so that we could learn (1) why each participant entered a certificate program, (2) how each person was employed at the time of entry into the certificate program, (3) what each person felt about the type and quality of instruction received while in the program, (4) whether the knowledge gained by participants during their studies later affected the practice of their occupations, (5) whether they felt that certificate programs have any unique characteristics, and, if so, how these affected their particular studies, (6) how each person was employed at the time of the interview and whether this employment was different from the previous occupation, and (7) if applicable, whether completion of the certificate program influenced this job change.

The sample for the study was drawn from lists of successful graduates of certificate programs offered at institutions in the eastern and midwestern United States, provided on request by directors of those programs. Care was taken to ensure an even mix of male and female respondents (three women and two men) and a fair representation of certificate programs that prepare students for employment in business and industry. Those interviewed included graduates of certificate programs at universities in major metropolitan areas, as well as those who attended a university program in a small city. Because of the distances involved, each member of the sample was contacted and interviewed by phone, the conversations taped with their approval. Although appointments were arranged with the respondents so that they had sufficient time and privacy to reply to the questions, none had knowledge of the questions prior to the actual interview.

Certificate Recipients' Perspectives on Programs

We learned from the participants interviewed that all but one had no prior experience with taking courses in a certificate program. Only the woman from the pilot study, who had completed the courses in correspondence fashion, had taken certificate courses before, and only in a piecemeal manner. Indeed, she had taken all of her certificate courses by videotape, in conjunction with many schools, and was pleased with this method of periodically receiving her "university in a box," videotapes that she played at her leisure while she supported a family.

All of the respondents sought out the certificate programs as a method of improving their employment potential. One man who was interviewed was working as a waiter in a restaurant at the time that he entered a legal assistant certificate program. He had been frustrated in his attempts to enter law school after his graduation from college, and he saw the certificate program as an avenue into the law field. For economic reasons, he needed to secure his qualifications for employment in a hurry, and he found a program in a metropolitan area that offered short-term, intensive study. He viewed the opportunity to work as a legal assistant as "a chance to know what a law career is about without the investment of three years of schooling."

One of our female respondents, who had not attempted any formal schooling after graduation from high school, was hoping to advance from her job as an accounting clerk at a small manufacturing firm. When her supervisor told her that the business was about to expand, he suggested that she look into a certificate program in production and inventory control at a local university as a means of improving her skills in an area of future need for the company.

We also interviewed a woman who had begun work in the food and beverage field in the mid 1980s. She felt a "desire to improve" in this field and turned to certificate courses in hotel and restaurant management offered by a university located near her place of employment. She mentioned that her superiors at work "were behind me going back to school," and that the support factor also influenced her decision to enroll in the program.

Indeed, among all of the respondents who were employed full-time at the time of their enrollment in a certificate program, there was a consistent thread of organizational support from their respective employers when they decided to return to school. The response of one woman, who told us that "the management of our company is very education-oriented," was repeated by the other certificate program participants that we interviewed. Although this support was apparently more often emotional than financial (such as tuition reimbursements), it is important to note that management recognizes the benefits derived from participation in certificate programs.

Once back in the classroom, the participants valued the "practical nature" of the classes and the "real examples" that teachers used in their instruction. The aspiring lawyer was among a group of classmates "putting together depositions by ourselves, doing law briefs, and really knowing what they should look like."

The woman who was new to the food and beverage management area said that her courses "taught me better ways of doing things." She also remarked that the practical applications of her studies to daily tasks gave her confidence in what she was doing at work.

The woman working at the small manufacturing plant learned "all the shortcuts . . . and hints of what to look for at work" and was thankful that the content of the certificate courses dealt with matters encountered each day in the performance of her job.

Everyone felt that the instructors' backgrounds as practitioners in the associated fields accounted for much of the real-world applicability of the courses that they took. One respondent mentioned that her instructor constantly gave members of the class "examples about situations that weren't in any textbook" but were necessary for successful completion of her duties at work.

The fact that most instructors were employed in the occupations on which they lectured also helps to explain their teaching styles, which our respondents found conducive to learning. Many participants referred to the open atmosphere in their classes, the greater frequency of discussions than of lectures, and the use of papers or case studies, rather than tests, as the primary means of evaluation. Indeed, one woman related the experiences of many of the students in a class where the instructor employed numerous tests and quizzes, a method that was apparently unsuccessful in many of the courses about which we inquired. All of the respondents gave better evaluations of courses in which there was minimal use of conventional tests in favor of discussions and written case analyses. It was apparent that the practitioners-instructors were more likely to use this popular style than were the full-time teachers.

Another aspect of the certificate courses that seemed guided, at least in part, by the nature of practitioners-instructors concerns the time of day when courses were offered. One respondent made special note that most of her instructors were fully employed in the same type of work that she hoped to perform, and that because of the work schedules of teachers and students, classes were held in the evening. The time of day that each class was held seemed to contribute to the accessibility of the courses to students who worked full-time during their enrollment in school.

Not all of the responses about the instruction were positive, however. In addition to trouble caused by excessive testing, it was found that poor textbook selection by instructors resulted in negative experiences in some classes. And one woman gave a poor rating to an instructor who, in her opinion, knew the material because of his daily work with it but had not taken time to properly prepare for his class.

All respondents were positive about the impact that the knowledge gained in school had upon their work. The former waiter gave us the most emphatic statement in this regard. After he completed the legal assistant program, he was hired to work in the litigation unit of a federal government department. Since that time, he has progressed to another position with a private firm. But, of his first position, he stated, "I couldn't have gotten that job without the certificate. That opened the first door for me."

The woman working for the manufacturing firm was promoted to the position of purchasing agent when she completed her certificate program. As she told us, "The boss was talking with me in 1985 about having me move over to do purchasing, so it was really good that I began to take these courses then." She now manages all of the purchasing and inventory control for the company, which has expanded since her promotion.

Many of the aspects seen by the students as unique to certificate programs have already been touched on in this chapter, namely, the practical nature of the course material, the teaching styles of the instructors, and the times of day that the courses were offered. One of our respondents also viewed the nature of the students in the program as a positive characteristic. As she said, "We were in class because we wanted to be, not because our parents or someone made us go." Another stated that she had been unsure of her direction when she originally entered college, but now she was able to pursue her goals through the certificate studies. This maturity and clarity of purpose characterized all our respondents.

One woman mentioned the need for better organization in the continuing education unit of the university from which she received her certificate. She believed that the school's "traditional" departments were more properly managed. But she had found little cooperation and coordination existing between traditional programs and certificate programs, resulting in what she saw as poor marketing of the certificate programs and a lack of conveniences available to those taking certificate courses. Examples of the latter included bookstore hours and administrative offices hours that did not coincide with the schedules of full-time working students. All of the respondents mentioned that their fellow students were quite vocal in expressing their opinions about shortcomings of the various classes. Yet, this one woman did not feel that the certificate programs at the school where she studied held a sufficiently high priority among administrative decision makers for adequate changes to be quickly effected.

Despite the problems mentioned, each successful graduate in our sample gained tangible benefits from their study in a certificate program. In a span of three years, the former waiter advanced from that occupation to paralegal work for a large corporate law firm, where he has been exposed to many aspects of international law and many branches and departments of the federal government and has worked in many major cities in the United States. He now contemplates reapplication to law school, believing that he has a much better chance of being accepted than he did earlier. He says, "I know that if I do go on to become an attorney, having been a paralegal will be so valuable. . . . I might still be a waiter without the first chance. The program helped me get that first job."

Positive Themes

In summary, our conversations with the certificate graduates revealed many strong points about the programs, yet, also identified areas in need of improvement. We found that enrollment in the programs examined was definitely work related. The people with whom we spoke pursued the certificate studies in order to secure better jobs. We also found that their employers valued the skills gained in the certificate programs.

Our findings show that the participants enjoyed taking classes taught by practitioners in their fields of study. The students valued the practical content discussed and concrete examples given, and they felt more comfortable with the teaching styles of these "full-time workers but part-time professors," who engaged their students in discussions more often than they delivered lectures and encouraged students to write papers and solve work-related problems instead of giving tests.

Perhaps most important to the graduates of the certificate programs were the career benefits that derived from the programs. The certificate recipients in our sample had all improved their work situations after completion of their certificate programs. Since many of the students entered the programs at a later age than the traditional college student, their career concerns were central. But we must emphasize as well the intrinsic value of the certificate to each of the people interviewed.

Challenges

On the negative side, it is apparent that there are drawbacks to employing practitioners as teachers. But, as we found in our study, the fact that the more mature students in the programs feel comfortable about pointing out such problems in their course evaluations should help correct some of these shortcomings.

More serious in our opinion is the peripheral position apparently accorded to certificate programs in comparison to other programs offered by the same institution. Whether the low priority of certificate programs is a product of philosophical or economic considerations, the fact that it mirrors the marginal role ascribed to adult education in general is a concern that must be addressed if certificate programs are to realize their full potential.

Thus, while the utility and popularity of the certificate programs that we studied were apparent, their benefits are not widely recognized. Only when more people in positions of authority in education recognize the value of certificate programs will their benefits be made available to the prospective students who can most profit from them.

Reference

Bogdan, R. C., and Biklen, S. K. *Qualitative Research for Education: An Introduction to Theory and Methods.* Needham Heights, Mass.: Allyn & Bacon, 1982.

Thomas M. Rutkowski is a doctoral student in adult education at the University of Georgia, Athens.

Margaret E. Holt is associate professor of adult education at the University of Georgia, Athens, and she is an associate with the Charles F. Kettering Foundation in Dayton, Ohio.

George J. Lopos is associate dean of continuing education at the University of Iowa, Iowa City.

The development of career certificate programs at George Washington University highlights one institution's pioneering efforts.

An Institutional History of Certificate Programs at George Washington University

Abbie O. Smith

This chapter provides insights into the development and growth of certificate programs at institutions of higher education through an examination of the innovative and successful certificate programs at George Washington University (GWU). In constructing this historical portrait, I discuss the reasons why and the manner in which most continuing education divisions of institutions of higher education began offering certificate programs. The conclusions drawn throughout the chapter are based on practical experience gained through experimentation with different program models over a twenty-year period. My conversations with colleagues around the country have revealed that many other institutions have enjoyed success similar to that of GWU in the implementation and expansion of their certificate programs.

GWU is an urban institution with eighteen thousand graduates and undergraduates, located four blocks from the White House in downtown Washington, D.C. In 1940, GWU started the Division of Extension, primarily to serve teachers in the school systems of Washington, Maryland, Virginia, and West Virginia. By 1950, the GWU's continuing education division began operations as the College of General Studies in response to requests by Washington-area organizations for educational programs in their own training facilities. The major constituent groups in the Washington, D.C., metropolitan area were then, and remain, local and federal government, the military, national associations, law and accounting firms, and area businesses (Lobutz, 1970). Employees of these organizations comprise one of the best-educated populations in the United States.

Early Use of Certificates at
George Washington University

The earliest use of certificates at GWU was to formally recognize successful completion of credit courses provided under contract to agencies, businesses, and industries in their facilities. Although employees earned college credits and grades, many had already earned an academic credential and did not plan to continue for another degree.

At the same time, GWU continuing education staff worked with university faculty to design workshops, seminars, and short courses in response to requests for employee training that was not part of existing credit course curricula or in credit course format. Since such programs were appropriately noncredit, the certificate became the accepted way of recognizing them. The value and recognition of the certificate as an indication of successful program completion began to grow.

Establishment of the Career Certificate Programs

Within the College of General Studies, a Continuing Education for Women (CEW) program office was established in 1964 to provide career counseling for women. CEW provided a resource to help women deal with economic hardship at a time of increasing inflation and high unemployment. CEW counseling staff were continually made aware that many middle- and upper-middle-class women lacked the confidence, skills, or contacts to compete effectively for jobs that would provide them a living wage in the Washington-area job market. The CEW counseling programs focused on helping counselees set short- and long-range goals with self-established time limits for acquiring the career skills, education, and experience needed to enter or advance in the career fields that they had chosen (Osborn, Smith, Parks, and Wolle, 1977).

A study of the educational attainment of counselees before they enrolled in CEW counseling programs between 1964 and 1974 showed that nearly 46 percent had completed a bachelor's degree, and approximately 5 percent a master's (Osborn and Strauss, 1975). Increasingly, the women attracted to career-counseling programs were interested in further education in order to become eligible for satisfying, well-paying jobs in professional career fields. Few training opportunities for midlevel professionals existed in the 1960s in colleges or universities in the Washington community. Those opportunities that were available existed through graduate degree programs.

First College-Based, Paralegal Career
Certificate Program

In 1971, an article appeared in a local Washington newspaper heralding a new paralegal career field and reporting that the Philadelphia Paralegal

Institute in Philadelphia was providing training. A CEW counseling staff member read the article and recommended the paralegal field as an ideal option for some Washingtonians. Since paralegal training was not available in Washington, CEW staff set up a series of meetings with local lawyers and with the GWU's National Law Center dean and staff to provide CEW with the background needed to develop the initial curriculum.

Washington, D.C., is an excellent place to begin a law-related program. The city is noted for having the largest number of lawyers of any city in the United States: one lawyer for every ten D.C. citizens (Sansing, 1990). A notice placed in the spring 1972 CEW brochure, announcing the planned start of a legal assistant program, generated three hundred requests for program information. From these inquiries, twenty-eight women and two men were accepted into the first class in fall 1972.

It was later determined by the staff and reported in the *Washington Star* (Seeber, 1980) that CEW's legal assistant program was the first comprehensive university certificate program on the East Coast that provided college graduates with formalized job training as legal assistants. The CEW staff and the GWU National Law Center administration shared confidence in the concept of the legal assistant program and enthusiasm for starting it. Faculty were drawn from the Law Center and the Washington legal community. The dean of the Law Center agreed to serve as chair of the Legal Assistant Advisory Board. The remainder of the board was made up of other prominent members of the Law Center and the legal community.

In promoting the availability of trained professional paralegals, CEW sent area law firms invitations to attend free workshops on ways in which legal assistants could improve the firms' legal services, heighten office efficiency, and save money for both their clients and their firms. Each firm was provided a packet of information that included copies of the curriculum, instructors' credentials, and resumés of students seeking legal assistant positions. The results were immediate. All of the students in the first legal assistant program class were hired before they had finished the program (Pinkus, 1983). It was an exciting time for GWU continuing educators.

Responding immediately to the success of the legal assistant program, the staff began searching for other fields that call for professional training and for which no university programs were available locally. The Center for Continuing Education for Women (CCEW), the first of several name changes for the unit, designed new programs and launched several each year after systematically studying Washington-area demographic data, investigating job opportunities listed in the local papers, listening to the career plans of hundreds of counselees, and giving serious consideration to dozens of proposals for new programs. Although some of these certificate programs did not survive, currently, fifteen different programs are successfully preparing participants to advance in their careers or to enter new ones. CCEW staff continually evaluate and revise the curricula to keep programs abreast of the newest developments in their fields. An advisory board established by each program director actively assists in this process. Some programs will soon be twenty years old, and others, newly conceived, will begin in the near future.

Current Career Certificate Programs

The number of elective courses available in each certificate program and the opportunity to choose from several major emphases depends on the size of overall program enrollments. An indication of program size, type of population served, and program longevity follows.

Legal Assistant Program, 1972. This program provides a broad-based curriculum focused on substantive and procedural law and the development of legal research and writing skills. The program has been approved by the American Bar Association since 1976 and is available in either a one-year evening or a one-summer intensive program. Over seventy students complete this rigorous program each year, and graduates are using their education in banks, insurance companies, corporations, and trade associations, as well as in law offices, federal agencies, and the courts.

Publication Specialist Program (Originally Writing and Editing Program), 1974. More Washington-area professionals are involved in publishing than in any other occupation. However, until the publication specialist program was developed, there were no substantive, local educational opportunities through which publishing skills could be acquired aside from undergraduate journalism and news-writing courses.

In the publication specialist program, students choose one of three certificate tracks: editing and writing, design, or production management. Each year, the ten-course program graduates more than forty people, who now hold positions as editors, writers, publishers, typographers, and printers, as well as advertising, marketing, and public relations jobs. Numerous other publishing colleagues brush up on the latest techniques by joining a class or two each year.

Landscape Design Program (Originally Landscape Architect Assistant Program), 1974. Washington, D.C., well earns its reputation as the "city in the trees" with its hundreds of tree-lined streets and many formal and informal parks. One of the largest urban parks in the world, Rock Creek Park, runs through the city and into the suburbs. The Washington area as a whole has large numbers of historic homes and gardens, embassy grounds, and suburban and regional parks. With examples of excellent garden design everywhere, Washingtonians tend to focus on their own yards, making gardening a popular pastime.

To serve these interests locally, there are many area landscape architecture firms, landscape contractors, nurseries, and landscape installation and maintenance firms. Until the GWU landscape design program was started in spring 1974, the nearest related programs available were a master's degree program in landscape architecture at the University of Virginia,

160 miles away in Charlottesville, and a master's in horticulture at the University of Maryland's Department of Agriculture in College Park.

Designed by the same team as the legal assistant program, this program was guided by a blue-ribbon advisory board drawn from the landscape architect, horticultural, and nursery business communities. The landscape design program trains those interested in working as independent designers to organize their own landscape installation and maintenance firms or to join the area's many nurseries, landscape contractors, or landscape architects. Thirty students complete the program annually. Redesigned several years ago, this is now the only CCEW certificate program that requires two years of course work to complete.

Fund-Raising Administrator Program, 1978. The practice of proposal writing for CEW built an awareness among staff of the art of fund-raising and grant-proposal preparation, and of the frustration inherent to these activities. The need for a substantive program to provide professionals with fund-raising skills for the nonprofit sector became clear. A program was begun in fall 1978 after many interviews with fund-raising executives in fields ranging from politics to the arts, sciences, medicine, and education. The fund-raising administrator program attracts not only certificate students but also numerous registrants who are not working toward a certificate. Approximately ten persons complete the certificate program annually.

Management Specialist Program (Originally Administrative Manager Program), 1980. This program was designed to provide vital management skills to individuals who did not plan to enter a master's degree program. Many of these students had already earned an advanced academic credential in a field other than business. As new managers, supervisors, or administrators, they were seeking immediate job-related skills and knowledge. The certificate helps students qualify as first-line supervisors or middle managers. Fourteen or more students graduate each year with a certificate.

Information Systems Program (Originally Information Systems Specialist Program), 1981. This program was designed to provide all professionals the opportunity to gain the computer knowledge and skills needed to understand and manage the information systems requirements of their respective fields. The information systems program offers three graduate-level certificate programs to meet career needs: information systems specialist, telecommunication technology specialist, and personal computer specialist.

The information systems program requires heavy investment by GWU in up-to-date computer hardware and software and the space to house them and is supported by two computer-equipped classrooms and a laboratory. Several generations of computers have been purchased since the program began. Because the computer field is always changing, first-rate technical personnel must be available to serve as instructors, teaching assistants, and laboratory managers. The program director also must constantly keep abreast of the changes in this rapidly growing field. This largest of the CCEW certificate programs graduates more than forty people each year and provides numerous professionals with individual courses.

Washington Representative Program, 1981. Through this program, students gain skills to serve as government-relations professionals and lobbyists for associations, political organizations, and corporations. Students new to the field can develop their skills, while veterans fine-tune theirs. Participants grow in their roles as effective representatives of their organizations by learning improved methods of gathering information, establishing contacts, and strengthening their ability to garner grass-roots support. There are few certificate course students enrolled in this program. Course enrollments by professionals who need expertise in specific areas but do not plan to complete a certificate predominate. However, only four or five students complete certificate requirements each year.

Public Relations Professional Program, 1985. Washington, D.C., is the third largest market in the United States for the public relations profession. Promotion of business products, government programs, and association services requires the expertise of public relations professionals. The public relations professional program has two tracks, one for students interested in entering the field and the other for management-level practitioners. Comprehensive training in planning, implementing, and evaluating public relations programs in profit and nonprofit settings prepares GWU graduates for the large and diverse community of public relations professionals in the D.C. area. This program has attracted large numbers of students who select individual courses of interest. Approximately ten student complete the full curriculum each year.

Childcare Directors Program, 1989. This program, developed in response to Virginia state regulations on childcare facilities by childhood specialists in GWU's Hampton Roads Center in Hampton, Virginia, is approved to meet the licensing requirements for experienced, qualified childcare directors and assistants in Virginia. A similar program has been started at the Crystal City, Virginia, Center to serve childcare directors in the Northern Virginia area. These classes are graduating between fifteen and twenty-five certified directors each year.

Desktop Publishing Specialist Program, 1989. This program prepares students for professional careers in electronic publishing. The program focuses on the technical skills needed to use state-of-the-art information retrieval systems. By also incorporating traditional publishing concepts of design and production, the program qualifies graduates to be administrators as well as technologists for the next generation of publishers. Participants are trained to use both IBM and Macintosh computers and the latest desktop publishing software. Expertise gained through hands-on file transfers and interfacing file format with layout programs allows the students to create portfolio pieces. The individual desktop courses are popular, and the number of applicants for certificate status is increasing.

Historic Landscape Preservation Program, 1990. This program is an outgrowth of a grant from the National Endowment to the Humanities awarded to GWU to research the extent of the need for preservation of historic parks and gardens and to develop a model curriculum. The program reflects the increasing interest among landscape designers, horticulturists, and historic preservationists in researching historic gardens and restoring them in an authentic manner.

Facilities Management Program, 1992. This program was developed at the request of and in cooperation with a founder of the International Facility Management Association. More than three hundred interested persons have requested information and fifty are currently enrolled.

Impact of the Certificate Programs

The impact of GWU's certificate programs in terms of contributions to the fields served can be measured to some degree by the size of enrollments in each certificate program. Size of enrollments is an important indicator of the value that professionals ascribe to the programs. In addition, through the high-quality instruction and technological sophistication of the courses, these certificate programs provide specific training for entry-level professionals and increase the ability of experienced professionals to contribute to their fields.

The foregoing certificate programs represent over nineteen years of program development and the successful matching of the interests of entry- and advanced-level professionals in various fields with the pertinent education, knowledge, and skills necessary to support those fields. Although these programs were originally designed to aid women in transition, more than 10 percent of the students attracted to these programs have been male since the first classes began in 1972. This development motivated another name change, from the Center for Continuing Education For Women to the Center for Continuing Education in Washington.

The efforts to provide educational programs to an audience of well-educated and sophisticated urban adults taught CCEW staff many lessons. Based on the academic community model, while incorporating more appropriate, nonpunitive grading and admissions policies, the following principles have well served the certificate programs:

1. When planning new certificate programs, choose career fields that offer professional, well-paying positions and provide opportunities for upward mobility. In providing programs for college graduates, program administrators must recognize that students expect substantive return for educational investment beyond the bachelor's degree.

2. Plentiful jobs must already be available or the need for trained people must exist if a certificate program is to have market appeal. Career certificate programs virtually guarantee success when designed to train professionals in fields where jobs exist but training for those jobs is not available.

3. An adequate pool of appropriately skilled faculty must be available. Recruitment of faculty from high-paying professional fields is difficult when adjunct salary rates are considerably lower. A large pool of potential professional instructors offers the educator a better chance to find appropriate faculty.

4. An advisory board must be identified and recruited. Advisory board members provide program visibility, future focus, faculty recommendations, and job openings for graduates.

5. The resources required to support the program must be attainable, and the project income-expense ratio must be in line with university requirements. There is no free lunch. Programs are judged by the excellence of their curricula, faculty, and students. However, to be considered successful, they must demonstrate their ability to return appropriately to overhead.

6. The program title should clearly indicate the profession involved. Efforts to attract enrollments in a program with a title that requires an explanation of the program's purpose are fruitless.

7. Job banks, referral services, resumé-writing skills, and interviewing techniques should be included as a service to all certificate students. The purpose of career certificate programs is to provide students the means to enter or advance in a field. Program reputations are built on the successes of graduates. Student services help ensure a good start for beginners as well as upwardly mobile professionals.

8. The career skills provided should be transferable to other parts of the country since most urban populations are transient.

9. The program should be unique in its content or delivery; it should not duplicate programs offered by other community organizations. Duplication of programs in some geographical areas splits the pool of potential students and may weaken the programs at the various institutions to the point that none succeeds.

10. Appropriate professional associations should be sought to endorse, approve, or accredit all programs. Collegial ties to professionals in the field strengthen the positive impact of the certificate program on the community and parallel the accreditation of degree programs.

11. Permanent student records and course data base files should be kept to provide grade reports and transcripts and to maintain administrative continuity. Recommendations from program directors, along with transcripts, constitute an essential service to graduates. Graduates also represent the best potential registrants for new course offerings.

Overall, as experience with the development of certificate programs grows at GWU, additional program criteria are formulated. Constant student, faculty, and advisory board evaluations help the staff to reshape entrance requirements, program content, and program structure to match the needs of each profession as well as the needs of the people attracted to the certificate programs. As fields become more specialized, different tracks are developed within the certificate programs to reflect this growth and specialization. Finally, by examining the critical tasks required of professionals in the field and by keeping track of job openings and how they were described, CCEW staff have developed the following program criteria to strengthen the programs and better equip the students for their chosen careers:

1. Substantive training requires a series of intensive courses that can be completed in one year of evening classes.

2. Entrance requirements of a bachelor's degree, letters of recommendation, on-the-spot writing samples, aptitude tests, and other proof of suitability are used to select applicants.

3. Participants earn grades for each course as proof of course content mastery.

4. A B average must be maintained. A student can repeat the course to replace a poor grade without having the original grade averaged in.

5. Courses must be taught by practitioners well known in their fields from the academic community, nonprofit associations, federal and state governments, and the private professional community. The breadth and depth of the instructor pool help ensure that courses reflect the newest developments in the field and provide excellent networking opportunities.

6. Students must develop and maintain a portfolio of projects in order to demonstrate their skills to potential employers.

7. Course and instructor evaluations following each course help program staff monitor student satisfaction and the relevance and articulation of the curriculum.

8. Program directors must maintain formalized referral services in the form of job banks or listings of job openings as an ongoing service.

9. Financial aid is made available through funds raised by benefits and through cultivation of donors. Although at CCEW only modest amounts have become available, the confidence that such awards inspire has encouraged many students to enter and complete programs.

10. The certificate-seeking group of students admitted at the beginning of the semester should be large enough that normal student attrition does not cause course sizes to fall to levels so low that the last several courses in the sequence become financially infeasible to run. After eight years of operation, CCEW allowed noncertificate students (those interested in less than a full program) to enroll, and they now represent over one-half of the CCEW student body.

Replicability of Career Certificate Programs

To be successful, certificate programs must reflect the areas of interest to the population of a region, as do CCEW programs. As mentioned earlier, the Washington area's largest employer is the federal government, including the military. Utility companies, colleges and universities, and the remainder of the service sector are next in size. A commonly heard Washington saying is that this community is dominated in the private sector by professions starting with the letter A: attorneys, accountants, and associations. Programs beginning elsewhere in the United States must carefully assess the special interests and major occupations of their own market areas.

Future of Certificate Programs

At this time, certificate programs are one of the most popular formats for offering comprehensive credit and noncredit continuing education programs (Lopos, Holt, Bohlander, and Wells, 1988). There are indications that programs of this kind are a long-term enterprise. The following trends illustrate why the future of certificate programs is secure within many universities, cultural communities, and employment sectors.

First, evidence of public acceptance of certificate education continues to grow. The Smithsonian Institution in Washington, D.C., now awards certificates for arts and humanities series that are not career oriented and yet are very popular: art history series, Asian civilization series, Western civilization series, and music connoisseur's series. Clearly, opportunities exist to build certificate programs around cultural activities that can appeal to populations in disparate locations.

Certificates that do not rely on large urban areas with plentiful and diverse employment and concentration of many specialized professional positions might be started in the small business or home business category. Required courses would provide necessary expertise in bookkeeping, marketing and advertising, business law, personnel practices, public relations, financing, inventory control, mail-order business practices, and franchise opportunities.

For locations with populations too small to support a course as such, internships or independent study could be set up for those interested in starting a business in a field in which their interest or specialty lies. Some of the following business entrepreneurships of a more vocational or technical nature may merit exploration: mobile, on-call auto mechanic; calligraphic arts specialist; writer and illustrator of books (such as children's, travel, cook, or garden books); clothing design and construction specialist; caterer and culinary artist (by region and by country); mobile, on-call computer specialist; garden designer; interior designer; mobile, small appliance repair; floral designer; food preservationist; wardrobe adviser; saleable crafts specialist; photographic/videotape family historian; interior design consultant; and home entertainment planner.

Second, increasingly, professional associations are recognizing the importance of certificate education and are beginning to formally approve college and university programs. As previously noted, CCEW's legal assistant program has met the approval standards of the American Bar Association, and the unit's counseling programs have met the accreditation standards of the International Association of Counseling Programs. Official association recognition of certificate programs adds prestige and leads to increased public awareness and acceptance.

Third, as the American population ages, increasing numbers of healthy older persons who are staying active in careers take advantage of certificate education. For such persons, certificate programs are becoming more popular than advanced degree programs; a certificate program is shorter in duration, less expensive, and more immediately applicable.

Fourth, there is a trend toward the licensing of practitioners.

Fifth, certificate education in some instances influences the establishment of university graduate programs, and graduate programs in turn influence the establishment of certificate programs. A GWU graduate degree program was started in 1986 in the same field in which a certificate program had been established three years earlier. The university's School of Business and Public Management now offers a master's degree program in association management, while CCEW continues its preexisting courses for association executives. Potential students can choose the program that better suits their needs. Those eager to earn an advanced academic credential will be attracted to the comprehensive master's program, while those who have already earned an advanced degree will be interested in making a shorter commitment, gaining practical job skills, and having the chance to develop the professional contacts that a certificate program provides. Referrals of potential students can now be made from one program to the other, based on which program is better suited to the applicant.

Sixth, despite such examples of collaborative referral, university faculty acceptance of certificate programs continues to be problematic. Although some faculty, numerous faculty spouses and dependents, and large numbers of university administrators enroll in certificate courses, there are at times noticeable tensions between university faculty and certificate program instructors and staff. These tensions are brought about by several factors: (1) Certificate programs have been offered on campus, where there is a severe shortage of classroom and office space for degree programs. Certificate programs will soon be moved off campus. (2) Few faculty are involved in teaching certificate program courses, although some serve on certificate advisory boards. Those who are actively functioning in the fields that they teach, and who would therefore be the most qualified to teach certificate courses, are generally very involved with consulting contracts and are rarely available. Faculty who are less directly involved in their fields are not attracted by certificate teaching, since more than half of the certificate students are already informed practitioners in the fields that they are studying. And (3) faculty have complained that certificate programs compete for graduate degree students in those fields shared by these two types of programs. Such complaints have generally come from faculty in departments where enrollments are down and where there is little contact with the continuing education program staff. The strategy of improving communications with the academic departments and offering marketing assistance has unfailingly benefited the enrollments of both graduate and certificate programs.

In writing promotional materials, continuing education staff make every effort to clarify the distinct advantages offered by both graduate degree programs and career certificate programs. Numbers of practitioners in fields served by both degree programs and certificate programs choose the latter because of the very close ties with opportunities for advancement in the practicing fields, their lower cost (at GWU, about one-sixth!), and the shorter time for program completion (about one-third). Other practitioners, particularly those who have not completed a master's degree, opt for the degree programs. Completion of either a master's degree program or a certificate program raises the quality of the individual's work life and increases the professional's ability to contribute to the field and the community at large.

Conclusion

From the beginning, the goals of GWU's certificate programs have been clear. Program administrators designed the programs out of concern over the lack of professional job opportunities in Washington, D.C., for the college-educated individual seeking to return to the job market. The staff designed the programs with a fundamental objective in mind: to provide high-quality programs to prepare graduates for rapid success in their efforts to find interesting and well-paying professional positions with advancement opportunities. CCEW has met this goal by providing up-to-the-minute instruction, creating job banks and referral services, fostering professional networking opportunities, and teaching job-searching skills, resumé writing, and interviewing techniques.

These comprehensive certificate programs have a highly visible impact on many of the individuals who take part in them. The atmosphere at graduation is joyous, and the success stories that quickly follow inspire the staff and spur them to continue their search for new fields in which professional training programs can make a contribution. The continuing education program staff takes pride that these programs enhance the quality of life in Washington's professional community.

References

Lobutz, J., Jr. A Historical Study of the Establishment and Development of the College of General Studies of the George Washington University. Unpublished doctoral dissertation, School of Education and Human Development, George Washington University, Washington, D.C., 1970.

Lopos, G. J., Holt, M. E., Bohlander, R. E., and Wells, J. H. (eds.). Peterson's Guide to Certificate Programs at American Colleges and Universities. Princeton, N.J.: Peterson's Guides, 1988.

Osborn, R. H., Smith, A. O., Parks, M. M., and Wolle, H. D. A Handbook for Admin-

istrators of Continuing Education for Women's Programs. Washington, D.C.: U.S. Department of Health, Education, and Welfare, Office of Education, 1977.

Osborn, R. H., and Strauss, M. J. *Development and Administration of Continuing Education for Women 1964–1974.* Washington, D.C.: Continuing Education for Women, College of General Studies, George Washington University, 1975.

Pinkus, S. "CCEW: On the Cutting Edge." *G.W. Times,* October 1983, pp. 5, 12.

Sansing, J. "First, Kill All the Lawyers." *Washingtonian,* 1990, 26 (2), 132–143.

Seeber, B. J. "Help Is at Hand for Women Who Want to Earn a Living Wage." *Washington Star,* March 8, 1980, p. C1.

Smith, A. O. *The Relationship of Age, Sex, Education, Experience, Income, and Field of Preparation to Job Satisfaction of University Career Certificate Graduates.* Unpublished doctoral dissertation, School of Education and Human Development, George Washington University, 1987.

Abbie O. Smith is acting dean of the Division of Continuing Education at George Washington University, Washington, D.C. She developed the Center for Career Education and Workshops, the career certificate programs unit of the division.

Certification programs by professional associations provide a cost-effective way for business and industry to address the technical development of their employees.

Certification Programs for Business and Industry

Theodore J. Settle

Business and industry address employee training and development needs through degrees, certificate programs, and courses by colleges and universities; internally sponsored training and development activities; and certification programs by professional associations. This chapter describes certification programs, which are developed and delivered by professional associations to further the image of the profession and to enhance the technical knowledge of their members.

Three similar sounding but distinct terms apply to training and development in business and industry: certificates, certificate programs, and certification programs. Certificates are documents with a diploma-like format that may be given to students at the conclusion of a training experience to acknowledge their attendance. Certificate programs are a sequence, pattern, or group of courses developed, administered, and evaluated by existing faculty or faculty-approved professionals (Lopos, Holt, Bohlander, and Wells, 1988). Certification programs focus on specific, measurable outcomes where individuals must demonstrate mastery of a body of knowledge. The individual acquires the knowledge through courses and job experience and is usually tested with an examination.

Certificate Programs by Business and Industry

Business and industry invest heavily in curricula and courses to develop the knowledge, skills, and abilities needed for employees to perform at a certain level of competence in their respective positions. However, the compensation and promotion incentive systems reward demonstration of this competence

NEW DIRECTIONS FOR ADULT AND CONTINUING EDUCATION, no. 52, Winter 1991 © Jossey-Bass Inc., Publishers

much more than completion of a prescribed series of courses. Therefore, participation in and graduation from certificate programs are less relevant in business and industry than in colleges and universities.

Certification Programs for Business and Industry

Although business and industry, unlike colleges and universities, do not offer certificate programs, they do make extensive use of certification programs, which address the continuing professional development of individuals in various job functions. That is, the focus of these programs is on the mastery of skills and knowledge by individuals already in a profession, not on the development of skills for entry into the profession. For example, many college-based programs in real estate and nursing prepare individuals for state or national examinations that serve as gateways to the professions. Once beyond these gateways, individuals can participate in continuing education activities to enhance their professional development. The Human Resource Certification Institute and Professional Secretaries International® are good examples of associations that offer certification programs to enhance the professionalism of individuals—for these cases in point, individuals in human resources and secretarial positions, respectively. Since few businesses and few colleges and universities have the resources to develop and deliver these continuing education programs, certification by professional associations addresses a significant need by employers and individuals in a cost-effective manner.

These professional development programs support individuals with positions in small and large companies across a full range of business functions (for example, marketing, manufacturing, engineering, customer service, finance, personnel, and quality assurance). The individuals may also be employed in narrowly focused businesses such as firms that specialize in financial planning, architecture, and real estate.

These related programs were comprehensive and represented the full range of functions and the more narrowly focused firms. After receiving and reviewing general information from seventeen nationally oriented professional associations, seven programs were selected for closer examination.

Certified Manager. The Institute for Certified Professional Managers, created in 1974 by a select task force of noted management educators and members of the International Management Council and National Management Association, awards the certified manager (CM) designation to individuals who meet their minimum performance standards in management based on their education, experience, character, and competence (Institute for Certified Professional Managers, 1990). The minimum education requirements can be earned through a combination of formal education and hours of supervisory or management training. Individuals can meet the minimum experience requirements through the length and level of their supervisory and managerial experiences. The character standard is addressed through three letters of recommendation, one of which can be a character reference. An examination addresses the competence standard and consists of three two-hour, multiple-choice tests in personal skills, administrative skills, and interpersonal (human relations) skills. Individuals can prepare for the examination by completing three intensive self-study or group study courses available through the institute on these three topics. (The courses take about forty-five hours to complete.)

The CM designation remains current for five years. The requirements for renewal and recertification are fifty hours of management education, which may include academic hours from a college or university, management development self-study courses, company-sponsored management development courses, management development courses carrying continuing education unit credit, and self-study programs approved by the Institute for Certified Professional Managers.

Certified Professional Secretary®. Professional Secretaries International® is a professional association of individuals involved with the secretarial profession. The membership generally consists of full-time employed secretaries and business educators (Professional Secretaries International®, 1990). In 1951, the Institute for Certifying Secretaries, a department of Professional Secretaries International®, developed and administered the first Certified Professional Secretary® (CPS®) examination to upgrade the secretarial profession by encouraging secretaries to raise their own standards of professionalism.

To earn the CPS® designation, individuals must meet certain education and work experience requirements and pass the examination. The education and work experience requirements are no formal postsecondary education degree with four years' experience, or an associate degree with three years' experience, or a bachelor's degree with two years' experience. The two-day multiple-choice examination includes a mix of questions designed to test basic knowledge such as facts, terminology, and dates; understanding of concepts, procedures, and principles; and application of concepts. The examination includes tests in six areas: behavioral science in business, business law, economics and management, accounting, office administration and communication, and office technology. An outline and bibliography acquaint candidates and educators with the examination. Individuals can also prepare for the examination via CPS® review courses or six review manuals and self-study guides. After passing the examination, individuals may receive up to thirty-two semester hours of academic credit according to recommendations from the American Council on Education.

The initial certification period is five years. Individuals can be recertified every five years through a combination of activities related to the CPS® examination or the secretarial profession, including formal academic course work at a college or university, seminars and workshops, employer-sponsored training, CPS® review courses attended or conducted, self-study courses, participation in construction of the CPS® examination, publication of articles, and Professional Secretaries International® leadership experience.

Certified Purchasing Manager. The National Association of Purchasing Management established the certified purchasing manager (CPM) program in 1974 to improve overall purchasing performance and to set guidelines for personal development of professionals in the purchasing and materials management field (National Association of Purchasing Management, 1990). CPM candidates must have five years' experience in purchasing and materials management or three years' experience and a four-year college degree, and they must have some combination of educational degrees, individual college courses, seminars and in-company training, work experience, and contributions to the profession. Finally, they must pass the CPM multiple-choice examination, which consists of four, ninety-minute modules covering the purchasing, administrative, organizational, and continuing education functions. Candidates can use the CPM study guide to assist in preparation for the examination. Individuals who successfully complete the examination are eligible for up to nine semester hours of academic credit at the upper-division baccalaureate level according to recommendations by the New York Board of Regents.

The initial certification is recognized for five years. Recertification requires participation in a variety of educational programs, publication of research-based articles, or service to the purchasing and materials management profession.

Clinical Specialist in Medical-Surgical Nursing (Certified Specialist). The American Nurses' Association (ANA) established the ANA certification program in 1973 to provide tangible recognition of professional achievement in a defined functional or clinical area of nursing (American Nurses' Association, 1990). The clinical specialist in medical-surgical nursing is one of twenty-one certification programs administered by the Center for Credentialing Services of the Division for Business and Professional Services within ANA. Individuals who successfully complete the requirements are called *certified specialists*.

Applicants for this certificate must hold an active registered nurse license, have a master's degree in nursing, have specific work experience, and pass an examination covering independent and interdependent client care issues and professional and practice issues. The multiple-choice examination lasts about four hours and requires knowledge and understanding of professional nursing theory and practice. Because the examination is practice based, ANA does not provide study guides. Individuals interested in preparing for the examinations should review the test content outline to identify areas needing additional study.

Initial certification is valid for five years. Recertification requires specific continuing education activities during the five-year period.

Certified Financial Planner. The International Board of Standards and Practices for Certified Financial Planners (IBCFP) was incorporated in 1985 to establish certification standards and enforce postcertification requirements (International Board of Standards and Practices for Certified Financial Planners, 1990). Certification candidates must meet four requirements: financial planning education, formal college education and/or experience, ethics, and examination.

To meet the financial planning education requirement, candidates must complete a course of study through a credit program, a noncredit program, or a self-study program that is designed for students at the junior level or higher and covers topics required by IBCFP. Typical undergraduate programs require 15 to 18 semester credit hours; noncredit programs typically require 180 hours of classroom instruction. The self-study program qualifies for up to 18 semester hours of academic credit at some colleges and universities according to recommendations by the American Council on Education.

The work experience requirement represents a mixture of formal college education and work experience in a position related to financial planning. For example, candidates without a college degree must have five years of work experience, whereas candidates with graduate education in financial planning may need only one year of work experience. The ethics requirement is met by disclosing any past or pending litigation or agency proceedings and recognizing the authority of IBCFP to enforce its code of ethics in accordance with its disciplinary rules and due process.

IBCFP publishes an examination content outline, showing the relative importance of 175 topics and the cognitive level at which topics are examined. Major areas of the ten-hour, one-and-one-half-day multiple-choice examination are insurance planning, investments, income tax planning, retirement planning, employee benefits, and estate planning.

The Certified Financial Planner designation remains current as long as the CFP licensee completes thirty hours of continuing education every two years and pays the annual license fee.

Senior Professional in Human Resources. The Society for Human Resource Management is the professional association for practitioners, educators, researchers, and consultants in the human resources field. An affiliation of the society, the Human Resource Certification Institute, offers the Senior Professional in Human Resources (SPHR) certification program (Human Resource Certification Institute, 1990). To become certified, an applicant must meet an experience requirement and pass a comprehensive examination.

The experience requirement represents a mixture of formal college education and experience as a salaried professional in human resources in either a practitioner, educator, researcher, or consultant role: undergraduate degree and eight years' experience or a bachelor's degree and six years' experience, or a graduate degree and five years' experience. The examination covers the following content areas: compensation and benefits; employee and labor relations; selection and placement; training and development; health, safety, and security; and management practices. The four-hour examination has 250 multiple-choice questions.

The initial SPHR certification is valid for three years. Individuals can recertify for an additional three years either by passing the current examination or through some combination of formal education, continuing education, research and/or publications, teaching, on-the-job experience, and leadership activities. Individuals who become recertified two additional times earn certification for life.

Certified Quality Engineer. The American Society for Quality Control (ASQC) established a certification program for quality engineers in 1966 (American Society for Quality Control, 1990). The certified quality engineer is a professional who can understand and apply the principles of product and service quality evaluation and control. Certification requires postsecondary education and/or work experience in a specified field, proof of professionalism, and successful completion of an examination.

Individuals can meet the education and/or work experience requirement by eight years of on-the-job experience in certain quality-related areas. Part of this eight-year requirement can be waived through degree completion from an ASQC accredited institution. For example, certification from a technical or trade school is equivalent to one year of experience; an associate degree, two years; a bachelor's degree, four years; and a graduate degree, five years. The professionalism requirement may be met through membership in ASQC, registration as a professional engineer, or signatures from two legitimate persons verifying the individual as a quality practitioner of the quality sciences.

The multiple-choice examination consists of two parts: engineering principles and engineering applications. The applicant must pass both parts, each requiring three hours. Applicants are encouraged to review the outline of the topics that constitute the field's body of knowledge and to concentrate their study attention on those areas that correspond with their least amounts of education and experience. The body of knowledge includes but is not limited to development and operation of quality-control systems, application and analysis of testing and inspection procedures, ability to use metrology and statistical methods to diagnose and correct improper quality-control practices, understanding of human factors and motivation, facility with quality-cost concepts and techniques, and knowledge and ability to develop and administer management information systems and to audit quality systems for deficiency identification and correction.

The initial certification covers three years. Recertification for an additional three years requires some combination of professional employment in the certifying field; continuing education activities in the body of knowledge; attendance at technical conferences, symposia, workshops, and section meetings; teaching of courses in the body of knowledge; publication of articles or papers in the body of knowledge; and other activities that maintain proficiency.

Comparison of the Different Certification Programs

These seven certification programs have four major points in common. All seek to enhance professions by developing the competence of practitioners; none provides basic entry into a profession. All capitalize on employees' internal motivation to achieve technical competence and recognition by professional peers. All require education and work experience in the chosen field in addition to competence in a body of knowledge, as demonstrated through an examination. All have recertification requirements of continuing study in the field and/or professional contributions to the field.

The programs have two major points of difference: availability and format of study materials and availability of college credits for passing. Five of the programs provide self-instruction materials to help participants prepare for the examination, and three of these programs also have materials for group study. Three programs provide a content outline and ask participants to concentrate additional study on potential areas of weakness.

Three programs of study were evaluated by the American Council on Education or by the New York Board of Regents and received recommendations that college credits be awarded to individuals who pass the examination. This feature is attractive to employers who are encouraging employees to return to school. It also demonstrates to participants who may decide to pursue an undergraduate degree that they can do college-level work and receive academic credits to reduce the number of hours needed to graduate.

Advantages to Businesses and Individuals

Certification through professional development programs by associations enables businesses to enhance employees' competence in specific disciplines or functional areas in a cost-effective manner. The programs are usually developed and monitored by experts in the field, with counsel from professional educators and test construction experts. The programs are highly focused and give attention to profession-specific content. They are generally short in duration, frequently available in self-instruction format, and usually priced to encourage maximum participation. It would probably be prohibitively expensive and quite redundant for individual companies to develop and implement these programs on their own.

Individual motivation to participate in these programs is generally quite high, since they tap individuals' interests in enhanced professionalism and respect through competence in the profession, provide national recognition and prestige, and enhance advancement opportunities (see Lopos, this volume).

Businesses encourage participation, primarily due to the quality of the content, but also because these programs require a joint investment and yield joint benefits. Businesses frequently reimburse an individual for examination fees and study materials; the employee provides the time, generally off the job. A business benefits when an employee acquires and demonstrates additional knowledge and competence; the employee benefits when he or she accomplishes both professional and personal goals.

Successful completion of a certification program indicates to the business that the employee has acquired competence over a body of knowledge, but maybe even more important to the business, certification implies a significant willingness by the employee to invest time and sometimes money in self-improvement. Certification also demonstrates initiative, motivation, and perseverance, three additional behavioral dimensions that are important to most employers.

Importance of the Certificate (Printed Document)

Higher education institutions and professional associations generally provide a graduate with a printed document, a certificate or diploma, to verify and recognize completion of a prescribed course of study or achievement of a professional certification. Companies frequently provide a similar document to the employee to verify and recognize completion of a curriculum or course and may place a copy in the employee's personnel file.

The primary value of the certificate is to the individual. He or she probably places greater value on a certificate for professional certification than on one for completion of a curriculum or course because of the recognition by experts within the profession. The certificate has less value to the employer because his or her interest is in the employee's application of the skills to the job, improved performance, and the associated behavioral dimensions that completion represents. In business, training is the means; performance is the end.

Looking Toward the Future

The education components of professional associations have not escaped the growing societal demands for accountability. Some demands have come from within a profession to enhance the capability and status of its membership. Other demands come from outside the profession in attempts to improve the quality of services. This latter group, possibly with a state legislative mandate to ensure public trust and citizen safety, has a strong consumer protection flavor. The aim is to hold professionals accountable for their actions, and education requirements often are the handiest means of ensuring that a person is equipped to continue practicing a profession (Eurich, 1990, p. 187).

The professions most influenced by these external forces involve individuals in specialty-focused areas or in medical and medical-related fields (Eurich, 1990, p. 188). Professionals in the first group include accountants, lawyers, and real estate brokers. Medical and medical-related personnel include doctors, nurses, nursing home administrators. Noticeably absent from these two groups are the majority of individuals in full-service companies with positions in marketing, manufacturing, engineering, and other line functions.

This trend of mandating professional certification for reasons of consumer protection raises several questions. Will professionals in fields susceptible to outside demands pressure their businesses for certification and the associated time and financial resource requirements? Will the external forces affecting some professions expand into line functions like marketing and manufacturing? Alternatively, will professionals in all fields begin to behave more ethically and responsibly to dampen the perceived need for external forces?

Conclusion

Certification programs by professional associations represent an excellent opportunity for business and industry to address the discipline or function-specific development of employees and for individuals to grow professionally. These programs do not exist for all professions, but they represent a quality, cost-effective way for businesses to augment their overall training programs.

References

American Nurses' Association. *Professional Certification: 1990 Certification Catalog.* Kansas City, Mo.: American Nurses' Association, 1990.

American Society for Quality Control. *Certified Quality Engineer Certification.* Milwaukee, Wis.: American Society for Quality Control, 1990.

Eurich, N. P. *The Learning Industry: Education for Adult Workers.* Princeton, N.J.: Princeton University Press, 1990.

Human Resource Certification Institute. Information packet describing senior professional in human resources program, Alexandria, Va., July 1990.

Institute for Certified Professional Managers. *Management Finally Gets What It Deserves.* Information packet. Harrisonburg, Va.: James Madison University, 1990.

International Board of Standards and Practices for Certified Financial Planners. *General Information Booklet.* Englewood, Colo.: International Board of Standards and Practices for Certified Financial Planners, 1990.

Lopos, G. J., Holt, M. E., Bohlander, R. E., and Wells, J. H. (eds.). *Peterson's Guide to Certificate Programs at American Colleges and Universities.* Princeton, N.J.: Peterson's Guides, 1988.

National Association of Purchasing Management. Information packet describing certified purchasing manager program, Tempe, Ariz., June 1990.

Professional Secretaries International®. *CAPSTONE.* Brochure describing Certified Professional Secretary® program, Kansas City, Mo., September 1990.

Theodore J. Settle currently owns a management consulting firm, Creative Partnerships, and for ten years was director of the NCR Management College at NCR Corporation in Dayton, Ohio.

When they are carefully designed, taught, and managed, certificate programs can provide quality education, access to new careers, and even social mobility to their graduates, while profiting the sponsoring institutions.

Certificate Programs: Alternative Ways to Career Advancement and Social Mobility?

George J. Lopos

Certificate programs are not new inventions, but their growth seems to be accelerating as educational needs are changed by new technologies and job redistributions within the nation's work force. In addition to summarizing the previous chapters and offering several other resources for information about certificate programs, this chapter considers the social implications of certificate programs.

The volume as a whole brings together for the first time a variety of perspectives on certificate programs. From matters of definition and history, to formal and anecdotal design considerations, to questions of profitability, institutional policies, and student reactions, this volume provides a comprehensive view of certificate programs as educational credentials.

The development of new degree programs is guided by a long-established tradition of educational principles and practices. Certificate programs, however, do not have such a well-established tradition. Thus, in addition to providing information about certificate programs, this volume, in keeping with earlier publications on certificate programs (Lopos, Holt, Bohlander, and Wells, 1988; Robinson, 1991), is designed to establish a literature that promotes the development of quality programs without decreasing their vitality.

What Is a Certificate Program?

The term *certificate program* is a confusing piece of educational nomenclature. In an effort to help clear some of this confusion, Holt (Chapter One) reintro-

NEW DIRECTIONS FOR ADULT AND CONTINUING EDUCATION, no. 52, Winter 1991 © Jossey-Bass Inc., Publishers

duces a definition that she used in an earlier publication (Lopos, Holt, Boh-lander, and Wells, 1988) and that appears in other publications (for example, Long, 1991). She traces the growth of certificate programs, beginning in the 1970s, but also notes the dearth of information or studies about them.

The advent of statewide mandatory continuing education doubtless contributed to the growth of certificate programs, but it also contributed to confusion of the terms *certificate, certification,* and *certificate program.* A certificate of attendance or participation in a conference says little about the participant's gained knowledge or improved performance. Successful application to a state or association certification board with appropriate substantiation of participation, and possibly a measure of performance and learning gains, yields a legal or quasi-legal status in terms of professional distinction or permission to practice in a profession. And, finally, a certif-icate program may involve both of the previous definitions or only one of them, but it does represent "a sequence, pattern, or group of courses or contact hours that focus upon an area of specialized knowledge or informa-tion and that are developed, administered, and evaluated by the institution's faculty members or by faculty-approved professionals" (Holt, 1988, p. 1).

The rationale for certificate programs as it has evolved nationally seems clear enough. Certificate programs are a response to the vocational needs of individuals and the educational needs of evolving fields in business and industry. The focus in these programs is on performance and knowl-edge rather than on the demonstration of accumulated knowledge found in traditional degree programs. Despite a difference in focus, Holt (Chapter One) indicates that certificate programs can possess educational quality in their own right as shown by the history of such programs at several institutions.

Quality by Design

The issues of quality is an acute concern when developing certificate pro-grams in the academic setting, especially since popular opinion may hold them not only different from but inherently inferior to traditional degree programs. The importance of this issue is apparent throughout this volume. Bratton (Chapter Two) and Walshok (Chapter Three) discuss the quality issue from two different perspectives. However, it is clear from both chap-ters that the key to changing common misconceptions of certificate pro-grams is to take all the steps possible to ensure program quality in design, faculty selection, institutional oversight, meaningfulness to the students, and administrative responsibility.

Bratton takes his approach from the field of instructional design and addresses the heuristics of certificate programs as guidelines for their plan-ning, delivery, and evaluation. To illustrate effective instructional design, Bratton chooses Kemp's (1985) thirteen-component instructional model as his guide to certificate program development. The ubiquity of Kemp's model is attractive for it can be used with any discipline and is as effective with traditional classroom instruction as it is with certificate programs. Bratton's chapter gives the reader specific formal guidelines for designing a certificate program. While not intended as a formula for success, Kemp's model lists design considerations used by effective teachers. Bratton's application of instructional design to the development of certificate programs stresses the need for deliberation and conscientiousness in creating programs, for quality in certificate programs ought to be a matter of design, not accident.

Quality Control from a Quality Circle

Another, less formal approach to quality control involves careful evaluation of the certificate program, its outcomes, and its political design. Walshok (Chapter Three) reminds the reader that the definition of quality varies depending on who is considering the question: faculty, students, or practitioners. As she points out, complications arise when notions of quality are "tied to the purposes and expectations" of degree programs rather than to the certificate program's own nature. These expectations deny that "certificate programs serve a different set of educational purposes."

Besides formal considerations, there is a need for great selectivity in choosing faculty to design and teach certificate programs—arguably, even more selectivity than is needed in traditional courses or programs. Evaluation by several sources is both implicit and explicit with certificate programs: students, employers, and certifying boards. The traditional indicators of quality—reputable faculty members and institutions—are not enough, especially when certificate programs are vocationally or task oriented; experience in developing and implementing programs is also important. Moreover, evaluation must be more extensive than just a few tests: The certificate program is best evaluated by measuring the learning gains of the students, including follow-up interviews with them, and by examining their rates of repeat enrollments in the program. When the results of program evaluation are incorporated into program quality, certificate programs can enjoy longevity and profitability.

Quality and Profitability

The economics of higher education are wonderfully abstruse! Even in this day of "bottom-line" thinking, colleges and universities support degree programs regardless of their ability to sustain themselves through enrollments or of even the most minimal indication of social relevance and student appeal. In short, traditional degree programs are not measured by their utility, whereas certificate programs are. With few exceptions, certificate programs must be profitable in order to continue, they must be self-supporting, and, in some cases, they even must bring profits to the sponsoring institutions. Robinson (Chapter Four) supports both Bratton (Chapter Two) and Walshok (Chapter Three) in their arguments for building quality into certificate programs, but she goes further by expanding on Walshok's contention that certificate programs can be profitable and educationally sound.

Profitability, for Robinson, goes beyond the narrow concept of program self-support and includes profit to the sponsoring agency, the student, and the employer. Is such profitability limited to a few select programs? Robinson suggest otherwise. She notes a 26 percent increase in certificate programs offered by Indiana University from 1984 to 1990, whereas there was an 11 percent growth of such programs in the state from 1983 to 1985. Together with the success of certificate programs on both coasts, Robinson leaves little doubt that there is a market for certificate programs and profitability in that market. Eurich (1990, p. 189) argues that mandatory continuing education has created a growth industry, "a lucrative and therefore competitive field for providers."

Besides the dollar amount of profit, certificate programs aid the university in other ways. Participation in education breeds further participation in education. This commonplace suggests that besides the money that directly supports the certificate programs, some students who begin with certificate programs subsequently choose degree work or further education. Where certificate programs serve as prototypes for degree programs, low overhead, contrasted with the great expense of developing degree programs, allows institutions to experiment without risking large investments of time and money.

Individuals who enroll in certificate programs also realize economic benefits. Robinson cites increased earning power for students with certificates that extend their knowledge and performance within selected fields, such as accounting (also see Rutkowski, Holt, and Lopos, Chapter Six). Higher wages and promotions are the most tangible economic benefits that accrue to participation in certificate programs; but when certificate programs introduce students to new fields, personal accomplishment combines with career mobility to the benefit of the student. Robinson's observations support those made by Smith (Chapter Seven) in her review of certificate program benefits for George Washington University students. As greater numbers of students and educational institutions perceive the economic value of certificate programs, more programs will find their way into the marketplace. However, colleges and universities are not the only sources of certificate programs; professional associations (for example, the American Institute of Banking and the Credit Union National Association) create certificate programs for their membership and for general use by business and industry.

Institutional Policies and Procedures:
Bridges or Barriers?

Does the success of certificate programs depend on the institutional culture in which they are designed and offered? Institutional policies, attitudes, and resources can encourage growth and experimentation beyond the tried and true; however, when policies are restrictive, resources are unavailable, and attitudes discriminate against all but the most traditional degree programs, certificate programs may still be successful, but only through strong individual efforts or inescapable pressures from clientele. Snider, Marasco, and Keene (Chapter Five) conducted an extensive survey of member institutions in the National University Continuing Education Association (NUCEA) to determine the extent to which policies and procedures affected the development and implementation of certificate programs. Most of what they discovered about policies and procedures at universities is inferred from the extensive survey of NUCEA member institutions, modeled in part from the survey instrument developed earlier by Lopos, Holt, Bohlander, and Wells (1988). The results of this NUCEA survey illustrate the traditional quality of most certificate programs: 76 percent traditional classroom teaching techniques, 59 percent daytime and 56 percent evening classes, with evaluation of participants by test in 72 percent of the programs and use of letter grades in 66 percent of them.

There is much in the NUCEA survey to suggest that certificate programs are traditional in their approach to education. But while their delivery and structure may be very traditional, their funding is less so. Certificate programs flourished where continuing education was self-supporting. Although this finding may indicate a lack of institutional commitment to the development of certificate programs, it asserts the ability of continuing education programs to take risks in the development of the more volatile and less mainstream noncredit programs for a rapidly changing educational marketplace. As a matter of policy at 64 percent of the institutions surveyed, certificate programs were kept separate from their credit counterparts.

There seems to be an interest in increased cooperation by universities with outside organizations in the development of certificate programs (50 percent). The enrollment requirement for 50 percent of the institutions offering certificate programs was a high school diploma, in itself a favorable sign that certificate programs can serve as entry-level access to postsecondary education. Snider, Marasco, and Keene indicate that certificate programs can be widely accepted on campus as long as their design adheres to traditional standards (see also Walshok, Chapter Three). If there is any desire to develop mobility (nationally recognized or standardized certificate programs) among institutions, the key to success seems to be the traditional design of programs. Strother and Klus (1982, p. 151) observed a decade ago that there was "very little standardization in the bases for awarding certificates except where the programs are linked to the licensing requirements." At least for the present, there seems to be little interest among the traditional universities to offer certificate programs as a major alternative form of educational certification outside of continuing education programs.

The View That Counts: Students' Observations on Certificate Programs

Academicians and practitioners can say what they want about certificate programs, but it is the students who enroll in the programs who offer some of the most important insights into the efficacy and personal worth of certificate programs as a mode of learning. Rutkowski, Holt, and Lopos (Chapter Six) conducted telephone interviews with five graduates of certificate programs from three different universities: a large, private, urban university; a southern land grant university, and a branch campus of a large midwestern research university. The students in these programs offered many of the same suggestions and observations made throughout this volume. Without exception, the programs provided access to career advancement, whether in a current job or through a career change. Although the students in their sample had various degrees of previous college experience, they all appreciated instruction offered by practitioners who emphasized practical applications of the materials learned. Each student saw the certificate program as worthwhile in terms of personal growth and career advancement. Coupled with their own vocational goals, strong support from their employers contributed to the students' motivation. Rutkowski, Holt, and Lopos's interviews bring to this volume what books on educational topics too often lack, the raison d'etre of all education: the views of the students who are learning.

George Washington University in the Vanguard

Smith (Chapter Seven) illustrates the evolution of quality certificate programs at a major urban university, from the certification of study in credit courses to noncredit programs designed to fulfill both social and employment goals. The history of certificate programs at George Washington University may well characterize the histories of programs at many other institutions where the programs were originally designed to aid women's reentry into the work force but became models of progressive educational programs for nontraditional students in general. The importance of the George Washington University experience is that it stresses the need for ongoing development and change if certificate programs are to have an enduring and relevant presence within the institutional framework.

"The Bottom Line" and "Where the Rubber Meets the Road": Metaphors of Performance

While most of the chapters here concentrate on certificate programs in collegiate settings, Settle (Chapter Eight) describes industry's view of certificate programs and seven association programs used by business and industry. Certificate programs developed by associations address some of the training and development needs of business and industry. The programs' goals are to enhance the images of the professions and the technical knowledge of the students.

The focus of these programs is competence and performance rather than just course completion. Among the seven programs cited, from the certified manager to the certified quality engineer, all seek to develop competence in the practitioners, require both education and work experience from the students, use the employee's motivation for technical competence and peer recognition, and fulfill recertification requirements in professional fields. Some of the association programs have recommendations by the American Council on Education or the New York Board of Regents for the awarding of academic credit, which suggests that the quality of these programs is comparable to that of the programs developed and offered on university campuses. Business and industry view successful completion of certificate programs as an indicator of additional knowledge and competence as well as a demonstration of worker initiative, motivation, and perseverance. For business and industry, the primary measure of the value of certificate programs is the development of competence, not the diploma, because competence translates to better products and services from employees.

Resources for the Development of Certificate Programs

During the preparation of Lopos, Holt, Bohlander, and Wells (1988) and of this volume, it became apparent to the editors that there is a dearth of materials on the development of certificate programs as types of academic credentials. A search conducted by me back to 1981 confirms the virtual absence of research and descriptive materials in this area. Most of what is extant deals with descriptions of specific certificate programs at institutions and certification programs in foreign countries. In general, what has been written about certificate programs in the past provides little information to practitioners interested in developing their own programs.

There are, however, several resources that may prove useful to practitioners as they consider developing certificate programs. Crispin (1976) surveyed 199 NUCEA member institutions about their activities in certificate programs from 1960 to 1974. This survey provides exhaustive data regarding the types of programs developed by the institutions and the trends suggested by these developments. Although the survey results are dated, the survey offers a historical context and methodology for someone interested in determining certificate program trends during the 1990s.

Roehl and Herman (1985) conducted a more comprehensive survey than did Crispin (1976) by mailing questionnaires to 2,367 institutions of higher education. The results of their study provide a variety of information about the types of certificate programs offered and some insight into the students who enroll in them.

Smith (1987) focuses on George Washington University's career certificate programs. This study's value to the practitioner comes from its detailed explanation of students' needs and experiences at George Washington University and the political history of how certificate programs developed in a traditional academic institution. Although the study focuses on an urban university, both the student and administrative experiences are sufficiently representative to provide guidance for the development of programs elsewhere.

Holt (1988) provides some guidelines to defining certificate programs. However, the main value of this publication to the practitioner is that it provides detailed information about fifteen hundred programs nationwide. Although intended for the student, this reference guide can give the practitioner a view of the types of programs offered by a variety of colleges and universities in 1988.

From the perspective of someone wanting to develop a certificate program, Robinson (1991) provides the most practical information: a step-by-step guide for certificate program development regardless of the type or size of educational institution. Robinson's suggestions are thoughtful and flexible enough to apply to a variety of programs and institutional settings.

Robinson's manual, together with the other sources cited throughout this volume, should provide the continuing education practitioner with enough information to start the process of developing a certificate program. Descriptions of individual certificate programs available in professional association journals and instructional program guides and directly from the sponsoring institutions, added to the information available in this volume, are a much-needed step toward increasing the availability of information about certificate programs as educational credentials.

Career Advancement and Social Mobility

American can no longer be described by metaphors celebrating the homogenization of cultures. The melting pot of our parents and grandparents has been replaced by today's salad bowl metaphor and a rhetoric of diversity that celebrates cultural identity and distinctiveness. Ironically, while extolling this new found strength in diversity, society is becoming increasingly fragmented into those with access to wealth, power, and position and those who are relegated to living on the fringes of economic and social advancement. In part, this fragmentation exists because of a discontinuity between learning and living, the consequences of which "may be described abstractly as civic crises—urban blight, poverty amid affluence, racial and generational conflict" (Hesburgh, Miller, and Wharton, 1973, p. 4). Despite political and economic attempts to reverse these growing divisions in society, education remains the single most pervasive countermeasure to growing social dissolution. Whether secondary or postsecondary, education must renew itself to deal with these "civic crises."

The foregoing chapters delineate a strong vocational and professional bias in certificate programs, although personal interest certificates are by no means lacking. Given this orientation, it would be easy but erroneous to assume that certificate programs are not among a university's educational responsibilities. Even our most traditional and prestigious universities are reviewing their roles in society. In its most recent manifestation, this reform has become marked by a search for the "new paradigm," an assembly of new models for the university's research, teaching, and service missions. Frank H. T. Rhodes, president of Cornell University, seeks to redirect his university's land grant tradition from rural agrarian to urban social "by shifting the focus of many of its experts in agriculture and rural development to examining the problems of urban poverty and pollution" (Grassmuck, 1990).

A redefinition of the university's relationship to society is a crucial part of this new paradigm. Undoubtedly, degree curricula and research agendas will receive more attention in this redefinition than will continuing education. However, certificate programs, particularly noncredit programs, can help redefine this relationship by placing opportunity within the reach of students who look toward the four-year institutions instead of community colleges or vocational schools for advanced nondegree education.

The record to date of this redefinition is largely inferential and anecdotal. Where four-year institutions have provided certificate programs, their success is in part attested by the students interviewed in Rutkowski, Holt, and Lopos's (Chapter Six) study, but it is also suggested by the numbers of certificate programs listed in and, unfortunately, overlooked by Lopos, Holt, Bohlander, and Wells (1988). Part of the problem of trying to determine the level of participation in certificate programs is that data on the subject are more readily available for credit than for noncredit certificates. Carpenter (1989, p. 20) reported that 4,267 post-master's and 6,661 postbaccalaureate credit certificates were awarded in institutions of higher education in the fifty states and the District of Columbia during 1986–1987. But the number of certificates reported is skewed because 4,352 certified life underwriter certificates were awarded nationwide by American College for Certified Life Underwriters of Bryn Mawr, Pennsylvania. Still, based on anecdotal evidence, it is reasonable to assume that this activity in the credit area is probably only a very small portion of all the certificates actually awarded during that period.

A new paradigm for the university's role in society will require the development of different credentials in addition to the degree programs for those wishing to extend their formal educations or seeking access to new fields. The student interviews conducted by Rutkowski, Holt, and Lopos (Chapter Six) are testimonials to the benefits of certificate programs for students seeking economic (and social) mobility. Whatever their personal motivations, from self-improvement to practical enhancement of job skills, these students and many others like them found new opportunities through certificate programs.

Traditionally, four-year colleges and research universities have left responsibility for vocationally oriented curricula to community colleges and vocational schools. If there is, indeed, a shift taking place wherein colleges and universities are reevaluating their responsibilities to society, then it seems to follow that they should also reconsider their position on continuing education certificate programs. This reconsideration is particularly warranted at state-supported universities and colleges, where giving taxpayers a higher return on their investment in the institutions may entail going beyond traditional campus-based degree education.

The benefits of certificate programs for institutions seeking to develop a new paradigm and respond to societal needs are significant. Academic curricula and degree programs do not easily accommodate the volatility of society's educational needs. Given the traditional process of program development, the time and cost to an institution of creating new degree programs in response to changing educational needs preclude such adjustments. Lost faculty development time and operating costs are not easily spread over the existing degree programs; rather, they are absorbed by tax support of public institutions or by reserve operational budgets of private institutions. In either case, the traditional, degree program development process is time-consuming and arduous, one not easily started or quickly completed. Certificate programs, in contrast, require less investment by the institution and its faculty (Robinson, Chapter Four) and yet can provide quality instruction (Bratton, Chapter Two; Walshok, Chapter Three). Clearly, certificate programs provide a logical avenue of response for an institution's new relationship to society.

While current institutional policies and practices do not reflect much interest in any but the most traditionally designed programs, persistence seems to be the watchword regarding certificate programs. A call for change in university credentialing practices was made almost twenty years ago by Hesburgh, Miller, and Wharton (1973, p. 76): "The university should study and, wherever appropriate, expand or otherwise modify certification alternatives for participants in degree and nondegree lifelong educational programs." The chapters in this volume make evident that the certificate program is an alternative with great potential for expanding continuing education programs while satisfying both individual career goals and corporate educational needs. Whether or not certificates can contribute to social change is less a question than a challenge facing colleges and universities and everyone who practices continuing education.

References

Carpenter, J. *Completions in Institutions of Higher Education, 1986–87.* National Center for Education Statistics Report no. 90–322. Washington, D.C.: U.S. Department of Education, Office of Educational Research and Improvement, 1989.

Crispin, E. A. "Trends in the Development of Adult Nondegree Multi-Course Certificate Programs." *Continuum: National University Extension Association Quarterly,* 1976, *41* (1), 23–34.

Eurich, N. P. *The Learning Industry: Education for Adult Workers.* Princeton, N.J.: Princeton University Press, 1990.

Grassmuck, K. "Toward the 21st Century." *Chronicle of Higher Education,* Sept. 12, 1990, p. A29.

Hesburgh, T. M., Miller, P. A., and Wharton, C. R., Jr. *Patterns for Lifelong Learning: A Report of Explorations Supported by the W. K. Kellogg Foundation.* San Francisco: Jossey-Bass, 1973.

Holt, M. E. "About Certificate Programs." In G. J. Lopos, M. E. Holt, R. E. Bohlander, and J. H. Wells (eds.), *Peterson's Guide to Certificate Programs at American Colleges and Universities.* Princeton, N.J.: Peterson's Guides, 1988.

Kemp, J. *The Instructional Design Process.* New York: Harper & Row, 1985.

Long, H. *National Survey of Certificate Programs.* Norman: Oklahoma Research Center for Continuing Professional and Higher Education, University of Oklahoma, 1991.

Lopos, G. J., Holt, M. E., Bohlander, R. E., and Wells, J. H. (eds.). *Peterson's Guide to Certificate Programs at American Colleges and Universities.* Princeton, N.J.: Peterson's Guides, 1988.

Robinson, J. H. *The Whats, Hows and Benefits of Noncredit Certificate Programs.* Manhattan, Kans.: Learning Resources Network, 1991.

Roehl, J. E., and Herman, P. A. *A National Survey of Certificate Programs in Continuing Higher Education.* Stout: University of Wisconsin, 1985.

Smith, A. O. "The Relationship of Age, Sex, Education, Experience, Income, and Field of Preparation to Job Satisfaction of University Career Certificate Graduates." Unpublished doctoral dissertation, School of Education and Human Development, George Washington University, 1987.

Strother, G. B., and Klus, J. P. *Administration of Continuing Education.* Belmont, Calif.: Wadsworth, 1982.

George J. Lopos is associate dean for administration and director of the Center for Conferences and Institutes at the University of Iowa, Iowa City. He is also adjunct assistant professor in the Department of English, University of Iowa.

INDEX

Accreditation, 6
American Banking Association, 33
American College for Certified Life Underwriters, 95
American Council on Education, 38, 81, 83, 93
American Institute of Banking (AIB), 39
American Nurses' Association (ANA), 80, 85
American Production and Inventory Control Society, 38
American Society of Association Executives (ASAE), 44, 45, 53
American Society for Quality Control (ASQC), 38, 82, 85
Association Management, 44

Bartensteine, S., 11
Beneficiaries, input from, 26-27
Biklen, S. K., 55, 60
Bogdan, R. C., 55, 60
Bohlander, R. E., 5, 9, 53, 72, 74, 85, 87, 91, 93, 95, 97
Bratton, B. D., 1, 11, 22, 88-89, 90, 96
Briggs, L., 12, 22
Budgeting: for credit programs, 35-37; for noncredit programs, 40-41

California, University of, 7, 25, 29
Carpenter, J., 5, 9, 34, 42, 95, 97
Certificate programs, 3-4, 9; by business and industry, 77-82, 93; common features of, 4; definition of, 4-5, 6, 77, 87-88; economics of, 33-42, 89-90; at George Washington University, 63-74, 92; history of, 44-45; interviews with students in, 55-60, 92; quality control in, 23-31, 89; quality and credibility of, 8-9, 88-89; resources for development of, 93-94; responses to, 6-8; and social role of institutions, 94-97; survey of, 45-53, 91-92. *See also* Certification programs
Certificates, 77, 88; importance of, 84
Certification, 6, 44, 88
Certification programs, 77; advantages of, 83-84; by business and industry, 78-

83; comparison of, 83-84; future of, 84-85. *See also* Certificate programs
Certified Financial Planner, 81
Certified manager (CM), 78-79
Certified Professional Secretary® (CPS®), 79-80
Certified Purchasing Manager (CPM), 80
Certified Quality Engineer, 82-83
Certified Specialist in Medical-Surgical Nursing, 80
Columbia University, 6
Continuing education (CE), 37. *See also* Mandatory continuing education (MCE); Noncredit certificate programs
Council on Postsecondary Accreditation (COPA), 46
Credit certificate programs, 49, 95; economics of, 33-37
Credit Union National Association (CUNA), 33, 39
Crispin, E. A., 93, 94, 97
Curriculum, updating of, 30

Economics: of credit programs, 33-37; of noncredit programs, 37-42; and quality, 89-90; survey findings on, 48-49
Education, 3, 49
Eurich, N. P., 85, 90, 97
Evaluation: in certificate programs, 29-30; interview on, 58; in Kemp's model, 16-17; survey on, 48, 50-51

Finances. *See* Economics
Frederick II, 44

Gailbraith, M. W., 6, 9
George Washington University (GWU), 6, 8; certificate programs at, 63-74, 92, 94
Gilley, J. W., 6, 9, 44, 53
Gonnella, J. S., 7, 9
Gordon, J. D., 6, 9
Grassmuck, K., 95, 97
Gustafson, K., 12, 22

Hankin, J. H., 3, 9
Hendrick, S. S., 7

Herman, P. A., 94, 97
Hesburgh, T. M., 95, 96, 97
Holt, M. E., 1, 2, 3, 5, 9, 10, 43, 46, 53, 55, 61, 72, 74, 77, 85, 87, 88, 90, 91, 92, 93, 94, 95, 96, 97
Human Resource Certification Institute, 78, 81, 85

Indiana University, 34, 38, 39
Institute for Certified Professional Managers, 78, 79, 85
Institute for Certifying Secretaries, 79
Instructional design, 12; examples of, 17–22; Kemp model of, 12–17
Instructional need, 13
Instructional resources, 15
Instructors: interview on, 58; recruitment of, 27–29; survey on, 51
International Board of Standards and Practices for Certified Financial Planners (IBCFP), 81, 85
International Management Council, 78

Keene, D., 1, 8, 43, 54, 91
Kemp, J., 12, 22, 88, 97
Kemp model of instructional design, 12–17; examples of, 17–22
Klus, J. P., 91, 97

Learning needs, 13
Learning objectives, 15
Legal assistant, 5, 57, 58–59; at George Washington University, 66. See also Paralegal
Licensure, 6
Lobutz, J., Jr., 63, 74
Long, H., 88, 97
Lopos, G. J., 1, 2, 5, 9, 11, 43, 46, 53, 55, 61, 72, 74, 77, 84, 85, 87, 88, 90, 91, 92, 93, 95, 96, 97

Mandatory continuing education (MCE), 45. See also Continuing education (CE)
Marasco, F., 1, 8, 43, 54, 91
Miller, P. A., 95, 96, 97

National Association of Purchasing Management, 80, 86
National Center for Education Statistics, 5, 34–35, 37
National Education Association, 44
National Management Association, 78

National University Continuing Education Association (NUCEA), 46, 91; survey of members of, 46–53
New York Board of Regents, 80, 83, 93
New York University, 37, 38
Noncredit certificate programs, 49, 95; economics of, 37–42

Organizations: and credit programs, 33–35; and noncredit programs, 37–39
Osborn, R. H., 64, 74, 75

Paralegal, 5, 39, 59; at George Washington University, 64–66. See also Legal assistant
Parks, M. M., 64, 74
Pearson, C., 43
Philadelphia Paralegal Institute, 64–65
Phillips, L. E., 45, 49, 53
Phillips, L. W., 7, 9
Pinkus, S., 65, 75
Pretesting, 14
Professional Secretaries International® (PSI®), 78, 79, 86
Proficiencies, 7

Quality, 23–25, 31; and appropriate methodology, 27; of core knowledge, 25–26; and curriculum updating, 30; by design, 88–89; and evaluation, 29–30, 89; of input from beneficiaries, 26–27; of instructors, 27–29; and profitability, 89–90

Revision, 17
Rhodes, F.H.T., 95
Robinson, J. H., 1, 25, 31, 33, 42, 49, 87, 90, 94, 96, 97
Roehl, J. E., 94, 97
Rutkowski, T. M., 1, 55, 61, 90, 92, 95, 96

Sansing, J., 65, 75
Seeber, B. J., 65, 75
Senior Professional in Human Resources (SPHR), 81–82
Settle, T. J., 1, 4, 6, 77, 86, 93
Smith, A. O., 1, 3, 5, 6, 7, 9, 63, 64, 74, 75, 90, 92, 94, 97
Smithsonian Institution, 72
Snider, J. C., 1, 8, 43, 53, 54, 91
Society for Human Resource Management, 81

Strauss, M. J., 64, 75
Strother, G. B., 91, 97
Support services, 15-16

Teaching methods: appropriate, 27; survey on, 48
Tillman, M., 12, 22

Walshok, M. L., 1, 8, 23, 31, 88, 89, 90, 91, 96
Wells, J. H., 5, 9, 46, 53, 72, 74, 85, 87, 91, 93, 95, 97
Wharton, C. R., Jr., 95, 96, 97
Wolle, H. D., 64, 74

Zeleznik, C., 7, 9

ORDERING INFORMATION

NEW DIRECTIONS FOR ADULT AND CONTINUING EDUCATION is a series of paperback books that explores issues of common interest to instructors, administrators, counselors, and policy makers in a broad range of adult and continuing education settings—such as colleges and universities, extension programs, businesses, the military, prisons, libraries, and museums. Books in the series are published quarterly in fall, winter, spring, and summer and are available for purchase by subscription as well as by single copy.

SUBSCRIPTIONS for 1991 cost $45.00 for individuals (a savings of 20 percent over single-copy prices) and $60.00 for institutions, agencies, and libraries. Please do not send institutional checks for personal subscriptions. Standing orders are accepted.

SINGLE COPIES cost $13.95 when payment accompanies order. (California, New Jersey, New York, and Washington, D.C., residents please include appropriate sales tax.) Billed orders will be charged postage and handling.

DISCOUNTS FOR QUANTITY ORDERS are available. Please write to the address below for information.

ALL ORDERS must include either the name of an individual or an official purchase order number. Please submit your order as follows:
  Subscriptions: specify series and year subscription is to begin
  Single copies: include individual title code (such as CE1)

MAIL ALL ORDERS TO:
  Jossey-Bass Publishers
  350 Sansome Street
  San Francisco, California 94104

FOR SALES OUTSIDE OF THE UNITED STATES CONTACT:
  Maxwell Macmillan International Publishing Group
  866 Third Avenue
  New York, New York 10022

OTHER TITLES AVAILABLE IN THE
NEW DIRECTIONS FOR ADULT AND CONTINUING EDUCATION SERIES
Ralph G. Brockett, Editor-in-Chief
Alan B. Knox, Consulting Editor

ACE51   Professional Development for Educators of Adults, *Ralph G. Brockett*
ACE50   Creating Environments for Effective Adult Learning, *Roger Hiemstra*
ACE49   Mistakes Made and Lessons Learned: Overcoming Obstacles to Successful
        Program Planning, *Thomas J. Sork*
ACE48   Serving Culturally Diverse Populations, *Jovita M. Ross-Gordon,*
        Larry G. Martin, Diane Buck Briscoe
ACE47   Education Through Community Organizations, *Michael W. Galbraith*
ACE46   Revitalizing the Residential Conference Center Environment,
        Edward G. Simpson, Jr., Carol E. Kasworm
ACE45   Applying Adult Development Strategies, *Mark H. Rossman, Maxine E. Rossman*
CE44   Fulfilling the Promise of Adult and Continuing Education, *B. Allan Quigley*
CE43   Effective Teaching Styles, *Elisabeth Hayes*
CE42   Participatory Literacy Education, *Arlene Fingeret, Paul Jurmo*
CE41   Recruiting and Retaining Adult Students, *Peter S. Cookson*
CE40   Britain: Policy and Practice in Continuing Education, *Peter Jarvis*
CE39   Addressing the Needs of Returning Women, *Linda H. Lewis*
CE38   Enhancing Staff Development in Diverse Settings, *Victoria J. Marsick*
CE36   Continuing Education in the Year 2000, *Ralph G. Brockett*
CE35   Competitive Strategies for Continuing Education, *Clifford Baden*
CE33   Responding to the Educational Needs of Today's Workplace, *Ivan Charner,*
        Catherine A. Rolzinski
CE32   Issues in Adult Career Counseling, *Juliet V. Miller, Mary Lynne Musgrove*
CE31   Marketing Continuing Education, *Hal Beder*
CE29   Personal Computers and the Adult Learner, *Barry Heermann*
CE28   Improving Conference Design and Outcomes, *Paul J. Ilsley*
CE26   Involving Adults in the Educational Process, *Sandra H. Rosenblum*
CE25   Self-Directed Learning: From Theory to Practice, *Stephen Brookfield*
CE22   Designing and Implementing Effective Workshops, *Thomas J. Sork*
CE19   Helping Adults Learn How to Learn, *Robert M. Smith*
CE15   Linking Philosophy and Practice, *Sharan B. Merriam*
CE11   Continuing Education for Community Leadership, *Harold W. Stubblefield*
CE9   Strengthening Internal Support for Continuing Education, *James C. Votruba*
CE7   Assessing Educational Needs of Adults, *Floyd C. Pennington*
CE5   Providing Continuing Education by Media and Technology,
        Martin N. Chamberlain
CE4   Attracting Able Instructors of Adults, *M. Alan Brown, Harlan G. Copeland*
CE3   Assessing the Impact of Continuing Education, *Alan B. Knox*
CE1   Enhancing Proficiencies of Continuing Educators, *Alan B. Knox*

U.S. Postal Service

STATEMENT OF OWNERSHIP, MANAGEMENT AND CIRCULATION
Required by 39 U.S.C. 3685

1A. Title of Publication	1B. PUBLICATION NO.							2. Date of Filing
New Directions for Adult and Continuing Education	4	9	3	-	9	3	0	10/11/91

3. Frequency of Issue	3A. No. of Issues Published Annually	3B. Annual Subscription Price
Quarterly	Four (4)	$45 (individual) $60 (institutional)

4. Complete Mailing Address of Known Office of Publication (Street, City, County, State and ZIP+4 Code) (Not printers)

350 Sansome Street, San Francisco, CA 94104-1310

5. Complete Mailing Address of the Headquarters of General Business Offices of the Publisher (Not printer)

(above address)

6. Full Names and Complete Mailing Address of Publisher, Editor, and Managing Editor (This item MUST NOT be blank)

Publisher (Name and Complete Mailing Address)

Jossey-Bass Inc., Publishers (above address)

Editor (Name and Complete Mailing Address)

Ralph G. Brockett, University of Tennessee, 402 Claxton Addtion, Knoxville, TN 37996-3400

Managing Editor (Name and Complete Mailing Address)

Lynn Luckow, President, Jossey-Bass Inc., Publishers (above address)

7. Owner (If owned by a corporation, its name and address must be stated and also immediately thereunder the names and addresses of stockholders owning or holding 1 percent or more of total amount of stock. If not owned by a corporation, the names and addresses of the individual owners must be given. If owned by a partnership or other unincorporated firm, its name and address, as well as that of each individual must be given. If the publication is published by a nonprofit organization, its name and address must be stated.) (Item must be completed.)

Full Name	Complete Mailing Address
Maxwell Communications Corp., plc	Headington Hill Hall Oxford OX30BW U.K.

8. Known Bondholders, Mortgagees, and Other Security Holders Owning or Holding 1 Percent or More of Total Amount of Bonds, Mortgages or Other Securities (If there are none, so state)

Full Name	Complete Mailing Address
same as above	same as above

9. For Completion by Nonprofit Organizations Authorized To Mail at Special Rates (DMM Section 423.12 only)
The purpose, function, and nonprofit status of this organization and the exempt status for Federal income tax purposes (Check one)

☐ (1) Has Not Changed During Preceding 12 Months ☐ (2) Has Changed During Preceding 12 Months (If changed, publisher must submit explanation of change with this statement)

10. Extent and Nature of Circulation (See instructions on reverse side)	Average No. Copies Each Issue During Preceding 12 Months	Actual No. Copies of Single Issue Published Nearest to Filing Date
A. Total No. Copies (Net Press Run)	1400	1465
B. Paid and/or Requested Circulation 1. Sales through dealers and carriers, street vendors and counter sales	162	42
2. Mail Subscription (Paid and/or requested)	724	760
C. Total Paid and/or Requested Circulation (Sum of 10B1 and 10B2)	886	802
D. Free Distribution by Mail, Carrier or Other Means Samples, Complimentary, and Other Free Copies	99	122
E. Total Distribution (Sum of C and D)	985	924
F. Copies Not Distributed 1. Office use, left over, unaccounted, spoiled after printing	415	541
2. Return from News Agents	-0-	-0-
G. TOTAL (Sum of E, F1 and 2—should equal net press run shown in A)	1400	1465

11. I certify that the statements made by me above are correct and complete	Signature and Title of Editor, Publisher, Business Manager, or Owner
	Larry Jabli Larry Jabli Vice-President

PS Form 3526, Feb. 1989 (See instructions on reverse)